VOCATION OF PEACE

Gordon C. Zahn

WIPF & STOCK · Eugene, Oregon

Wipf and Stock Publishers
199 W 8th Ave, Suite 3
Eugene, OR 97401

Vocation of Peace
By Zahn, Gordon C.

ISBN 13: 978-1-60899-052-8
Publication date 4/26/2010
Previously published by Fortkamp -- Cath Worker, 1992

FOR

PAUL HANLY FURFEY and DOROTHY DAY

who lighted the torch

and for MICHAEL HOVEY and all the others

who will keep its flame bright

CONTENTS

INTRODUCTION

October 1992 marks the fiftieth anniversary of my official entry into the "Catholic peace movement" when I reported for my Civilian Public Service duty at Warner, N.H. I had been giving talks against the then impending World War II for a number of years, but when I was picked up at the Warner rail station it was the first time I had met another Catholic who shared my conscientious objection. To call it a "movement" is to stretch a point, of course. What I found at Warner was a number of extremely independent characters representing almost an equal number of different positions against the war and united only in their common rejection of military service. The camp was sponsored by a Catholic Worker "front" — the Association of Catholic Conscientious Objectors — and administered by former CW staffers. Nevertheless the peace commitment of most campers (including my own) did not carry over into commitment to the CW movement as such or its program and principles.

The past fifty years have accounted for many changes, but few have been as great as the awakening to the pacifist implications of their faith on the part of Roman Catholics and, more significant, the institutional Church. Today Pax Christi USA, the leading American manifestation of that change, can claim a growing membership in the neighborhood of 10,000 *including almost 100 bishops* — and it is only one of more than two dozen sections comprising Pax Christi International. That I have contributed in some small fashion to the development of both and, through them and other associations, to the re-discovery of peace traditions tracing back to the earliest days of Christianity is a source of no small pride.

This selection from articles written over this span of years was not easy. The temptation to choose my "all-time favorites" or "golden oldies" was strong, but I decided some might not have sufficient meaning or relevance for readers today and, besides, several I might have included had already been published in an earlier collection (*War, Conscience and Dissent* (1967) — could that have been 25 years ago?). And, of course, most of those I did choose can qualify as personal "favorites" anyway.

Instead, this is more of a "theme" collection, the theme set forth in the title of the opening selection and of the volume itself. Its underlying premise is that *all* Christians, whether they realize it or not, have that "vocation" (*in the full religious sense*) of serving the cause of peace and, by logical extension, the obligation to oppose war and any support or participation in war. The profession was made by us or for us at baptism committing us — as "other Christs," not merely "imitators of Christ" — to continue His witness of nonviolent love, and this profession became a commitment to action at confirmation. In Thomas Merton's words, "He brought to his disciples a vocation and a task, to struggle in a world of violence to establish His peace not only in their own hearts but in society itself." The gains that have been made over the past fifty years must not obscure the fact that there is much more to be done. The struggle is far from over.

The first section sets forth the theme putting particular emphasis on the role of conscience and the moral responsibility conscience defines for the Christian.

Its promptings represent our understanding of what God requires of us, and are to be translated into personal behavior in order that we may become an effective "witness" to Him. The essays in the second section may seem peripheral to war and conscientious objection; but they, too, deal with issues that are related to the general theme and present (or have presented) special difficulties often leading to confusion, sometimes failure, in reconciling them with our moral obligations in other areas of moral concern.

Finally, the third section features examples of individuals or groups who have witnessed to peace in different ways, examples having special meaning for me personally. Some will be unfamiliar to readers; some perhaps dubious choices in their judgment. As I see it, however, all of them deserve recognition for accepting the challenge of the vocation of peace and at least attempting to meet that challenge by following the guidance provided by their individual consciences.

I would describe my approach as "sociotheological," a term which may upset theologian and sociologist alike as well as frighten the ordinary reader. It could offend specialists in both camps by introducing a linkage each regards as an intrusion: the theologian objecting to the implication that moral teachings and traditions should be tested against actual social behavior of those who profess them and my fellow sociologists decrying the violation of their ideal of a "value-free" science. As for the innocent bystanders who have been spared immersion in either discipline, they may fear (with some justice) being subjected to the ostentatiously precise terminology ("jargon") and the stress on overly intricate distinctions to which both are too often prone. Such readers may take some comfort in the fact that most of these selections were published in general, not scholarly, publications. My justification of the linkage is relatively simple. If the "vocation" is defined by religious values, these should be traceable in the believer's perceptions, motivations, and behavior and be given expression in the believer's social relationships. To divorce either from the other invites the kind of behavioral compartmentalization that accounts for the scandal of Christians fighting and killing other Christians in almost every major war in history. It is the task of the vocation of peace to combine the moral insights and objectives of theology with the behavioral insights and potential provided by sociology (and the other social sciences as well) if it is to reach its goal, the elimination of war.

At first it was my intention to present these selections unchanged from their original publication. It soon became obvious that this would not work. Some of the references were too "time-bound" to be fully meaningful to the contemporary reader. However, whatever editing has been done (to avoid undue repetition, to improve style through minor changes in grammar, etc.) does not change the substance, argument, or relevant content of the article. In other words, there are no "second thoughts" to modify or "correct" positions taken. One final note: the primary focus is consistently upon the Catholic Church and the behavioral record of its members.

The reason for this lies in my personal conviction that, as a loyal participant in that religious community, I have an obligation to do everything I can to make of it the most effective vehicle for promoting the vocation of peace. If, at times, this may call for criticism ("fraternal correction" is probably the preferred term) or even a kind of "conversion" effort, that can become part of my performance of that vocation. But to maintain this particularity of emphasis certainly does not restrict these selections to the Catholic audience. The focus may be there, but much of what is said can relate as well to the broader *Christian* religious community — and, even beyond that, to "all men and women of good will" to whom the beloved Pope John XXIII addressed his encyclical, "Peace on Earth."

Attempts to "convert" the Church or "keep her honest" on questions relating to moral implications of social behavior have not always been welcomed and almost certainly will not be welcomed in the future. That, along with whatever unpleasantness that may bring, is also part of that vocation of peace. When we consider the great changes that have taken place in the past fifty years, credit is due to a relative few — "maverick" bishops like Archbishop T.D. Roberts, S.J., of England, "way-out" radical priests like the Berrigans, and "rebellious" laypersons like a Franz Jaegerstaetter — who may have been ignored or even ridiculed (if not disciplined and condemned) for keeping the issues of pacifism, conscientious objection, and the like alive when considerations of "prudence" or "orthodoxy" advised silence.

It would be presumptuous to claim that the few essays in this volume played much of a part in demonstrating the need for the "entirely new attitude" called for by the Second Vatican Council. But as part of the active and still growing "Catholic peace movement" they may have contributed to what George Weigel deplores as the "abandonment of the heritage" (meaning the "just war" tradition). In his book, *Tranquillitas Ordinis*, Weigel does me the great honor of identifying me — along with Dorothy Day, Thomas Merton, the Berrigans, and James Douglass — as bearing a share of the responsibility for that "abandonment." If he is right, I take some gratification from knowing my fifty years have not been wasted.

1.
The Christian Vocation of Peace

The topic may not sound as "subversive" or, for that matter, "heretical" as it did for many Catholics a half-century ago when my application for deferment from military service as a conscientious objector was being considered by a Milwaukee draft board. There may still be priests here and there who insist (as one did at my hearing) that it was impossible for a Catholic to take that stand; but it is now easy to quote bishops, even popes, to set the record straight.

Which is not to say, however, that the Catholic Church can now be classified as "a peace church" or that all Catholics accept and follow the guidance offered by those bishops and popes. One of our major archdioceses has found it advisable to substitute "social concerns" for "peace" in what was formerly its "Justice and Peace Commission" — to avoid the unfavorable implications some might attach to the P-word. And when it comes to conscientious objection, even John Paul II's reference to it as "a sign of maturity" may not be enough to establish its legitimacy for the men and women in the pews (or, for that matter, in the sacristy).

To speak of peace as a vocation for the Christian implies more than merely accepting it as preferable to a state of violent conflict, more even than the subject of pious prayer. Both are appropriate, of course, but it must not stop at that. The first essential step in fulfilling that vocation is a firm rejection of war and all that makes for war. Twenty-five years ago Cardinal Alfrink, then President of Pax Christi International, told a meeting of Dutch military chaplains, "The existence of nuclear weapons excludes the existence of a just war, because the means that could be used to fight injustice would cause much greater injustice."

Ten years ago John Paul II went further to declare, "Today the scale and the horror of modern warfare — whether nuclear or not — makes it totally unacceptable as a means of settling differences between nations." Since then U.S. armed forces have been engaged in combat in Grenada, Panama, and, most recently, the Persian Gulf. Though a growing number of Catholics — including in the latter case, a number of outspoken bishops — have opposed these wars, Catholics still represent a major segment of those forces.

The technological horrors of today's weaponry, coupled with the strategies for which they were designed, have reduced warfare to a test of rival killing machines. It was always that to some extent, of course, but in the past the machines were under the control of human beings. Today the reverse may be true. I recall a television newscast dealing with National Guard training procedures in which the officer being interviewed was positioned before a wall poster bearing the legend, "No war was ever won with compassion or conscience . . . KILL." The wonders of our new military technology represent a more efficient application of that dubious principle. The billboard overlooking Tulagi Bay in World War II ("Kill Japs . . . Kill Japs . . . Kill More Japs") would be sadly out of date. The machines already are set for that, and once the button is pressed, they need no "psyching-up," nor are they subject to aftereffects of psychological remorse.

This presents a problem for theologians working their side of the equation. It is their task to find or create new qualifications and ambiguities to somehow stretch the "just war" concessions introduced by Augustine and developed by others over the 1600 years that theory has been "in possession," as the U.S. bishops put it in their 1983 pastoral letter. Once they wake up to the fact that it really cannot be done (at least not with a straight face) it will become obvious to all that the genius of war and the genius of Christianity are irreconcilable; that acceptance of the one necessarily precludes any possibility of full commitment to the other. The Christian will be faced with a crisis of conscience, forced to decide which of the two contending masters is to be served.

One may assume this tension will be present during any war, but for the most part the Christian called to participate in war or support those who do may find it "resolved" before that moral choice reaches the psychological crisis threshold. Throughout history the resolution has taken the form of "spiritual" dedication to, in the one case, sacrifice for a greater good or, in another, the crusader's quest for glory and eternal reward. Seen in this light, even the most lethal and destructive acts of war are given an overlay of spiritual worth.

Meritorious and soul-satisfying though such intentions and declarations may be in their own right, the moral dilemma posed by war, especially modern war, is more frequently resolved in favor of "the world" and its practical concern for national survival. Christians have become so deeply enmeshed in the social milieu and their activities so dominated by existential needs that the spiritual dimension of normal everyday behavior is not recognized. In past research with Royal Air Force chaplains, for example, I raised the question of how they would deal with certain clearly immoral orders or acts of war. After presenting a number of "hypothetical" cases (which, unfortunately have happened much too often), several confessed they had never given any thought at all to the possibility that such situations might arise or how they might react to them if they did.

For those Catholics who do experience the moral tensions and even the hint of the crisis of conscience they should impose, there is always the escape hatch offered by the process of "compartmentalization," relegating moral and spiritual concerns to strictly defined and limited times and places. The convenient "out" this provides may be chosen, but it does not meet the test of an active Christian commitment. The phenomenon of war, if it is nothing else, is an open denial of the presumed universal brotherhood and sisterhood of all human beings under the care and authority of a loving personal God. The familiar exhortations and counsels to "resist not the evildoer," "turn the other cheek," "love thy neighbor" (and *enemy* as well!) are superseded by a completely contrary set of directives and orders as that attributed to an American officer leading his unit into a Vietnamese village: "Kill them! I don't want anything moving."

Stanley Windass (*Christianity Versus Violence,* 1964) has shown that the earliest Christians clearly recognized that theirs was a vocation for peace — in the pacifist sense, not in the euphemisms of the Strategic Air Command's "peace is our profession" slogan and the other products of Pentagon public relations expertise. He cites Origen's warning to beware lest "for warfare, or for the vindication of our rights, or for any occasion we should take the sword, for no such occasion is allowed by this evangelical teaching." Windass counters the argument that this was an extreme or exceptional case by noting, "All the evidence suggests, on the contrary, that this was the only stream of thought — though not the only stream of practice."

There were Christians who served in the imperial forces, but they were the theological deviants of their day. Later centuries witnessed a reversal which found eminent theologians introducing and elaborating upon the concept of a "just" war and popes preaching violent crusades. Nevertheless, Christian pacifism, however much a minority or deviant position it may have become, was never extinguished altogether. The element of tension was always present. War, even when "justified," was always regarded as evil though all too easily described as a "lesser" or "necessary" evil to enable the Christian called to serve and kill in war to resolve whatever moral tension there may have been.

If, as the pacifist holds, the concept of war and its practices are "alien" to Christian teaching and belief, any definition of the role of the Christian called to the vocation of peace begins with the rejection of war and violence. "If possible, so far as it lies with you, live at peace with all men" is to be read as an instruction, not as a pious hope. The first priority is to make oneself and others more aware, not less, of the tension between their spiritual and worldly needs and duties so that the former can be assured of priority it deserves in the resolution of that tension. This is much easier to state as the objective, of course, than to accept as a definite program of action.

We must stop glamorizing war and men (now women too!) at war. The episodes of heroic self-sacrifice that do occur will continue to stir admiration, but we should remember that the more characteristic events of a military campaign are likely to be acts of wanton, sometimes obscene, brutality. Consider, for example, the picture of grinning British soldiers gathered around one of their number holding the severed head of an enemy by the hair; the televised matter-of-fact kick sending the corpse of a captive who had just been tortured to death rolling into a convenient ditch; the exultant boast of the American pilot for whom the opportunity to "go out and get" himself a VC in Vietnam "makes his day"; more recently, the body fragments strewn along the "highway of death" in Iraq.

Reports like these are encountered frequently in the daily press and TV coverage, but they seldom are found in the pages of our religious press. Nor does one find the slightest hint that this is the way wars are fought and won today in laudatory statements of religious leaders memorializing the sacrifices of the armed forces. Until we insist that it is not the proper role of Christ's church or its ministers to make war, to bless war, or even to praise war and the deeds of war, we will never be able to bring the full measure of dedication and spirit to the Christian vocation of peace.

National flags should be removed from our churches; the touches of chauvinistic fervor that often flavors sermons and ceremonials should be dropped; the military training that has become a part of the curriculum of Catholic colleges and universities (now some high schools too!) should be eliminated. Once we are freed from the uncritical acceptance of the legitimacy and merit of the military calling we may make more and faster progress in our efforts to bring peace to the world. But not before.

We must stop boasting that, come what may, the Christian will always be the best patriot and recognize instead that the true Christian must always set some limits to his patriotic commitment, even to the point of being prepared to risk the defeat of his nation if the only alternative is the serious violation of God's law.

These are only preliminaries. No longer "conditioned" from childhood on to unquestioningly accept military service as a permissible, even praiseworthy, activity, the Christian will be forced to make an independent moral evaluation and judgment concerning any war he or she may be called upon to fight or support. The formation of the consciences of young people with respect to the moral teachings on war and peace must become a major responsibility of the religious community and all its agencies. Only then can we expect the individual to be prepared to make a valid moral decision on the basis of facts available, taking into account all the interpretations of those facts deserving consideration. The pragmatics of temporal and national imperatives must be considered but should not be given absolute priority in the final decision. There are broader and more far-reaching concerns to be weighed: the needs of the international order; the rights of those to be designated as "enemy"; and, above all, supernatural values along with their implications for reward and punishment in the hereafter.

The formation of a sound conscience, like the saving of one's soul, is an essential minimum for the Christian, but it is not enough. Part of the mission for bringing peace to the world is to assist others to do the same. One reviewer of my study of German Catholic support for Hitler's wars took issue with my position that the German bishops had an obligation to warn their faithful about the possible injustice and immorality of the war. "Why," he (a priest no less) asked, "should the conscience once formed be disturbed?" Given the distinction between "formal" and "material" sin, there may be some point to the question. Still, even making allowance for that, another consideration must also be taken into account: the protection of the innocent who might be slaughtered by the individual (a Catholic!) acting according to an undisturbed but erroneous conscience. Certainly it offers small comfort to the victims and survivors of what Paul VI called the "infernal massacre" of Hiroshima to know that those responsible for that atrocity were probably acting in good faith and guilty of no more than material sin.

Those who did question the morality of the Hiroshimas and the Dresdens of World War II but remained silent also failed dismally as Christians. Even were there no one to listen — and certainly no one to follow — the Christian who is alert to the moral imperatives of a situation has a responsibility to make them known. This was the problem posed by Rolf Hochhuth in his controversial play about Pius XII. One may reject his distortion of the Pope's character and motivation, but the basic challenge cannot be dismissed or ignored. Pius had knowledge of the Holocaust and did not issue any public condemnation. The question is not whether the Nazis (or anyone else) would have taken note of a papal protest, not even whether Jews would have been saved. What should have been a far more important consideration was the loyal German Catholics who never questioned the moral rightness or wrongness of what their government was saying and doing about the Jews, who may even have participated in the extermination program somewhere along the line.

So, too, with this nation's war in Vietnam. The question was not whether the Johnson Administration paid attention to the religiously motivated protests against the war, whether such protests ever held real promise of stopping the excesses being perpetrated, or whether those who actually unleashed the napalm and the insidious fragmentation bombs were aware of the immorality of "area destruction" weapons declared by Vatican II and followed orders nonetheless. A more troubling question was whether Christians who were aware of the moral evil of such acts and of the war itself saw it as part of their vocation for peace to make their misgivings known and try to "trouble" as many consciences as possible.

The Christian who accepts the personal obligation to discover and pursue the pacifist implications of the faith and awaken others to them as well has yet another obligation. Everything must be done to make certain, as far as possible, that the actions taken to oppose the evil earn and receive the respectful hearing they deserve from others who continue to differ with them. It goes without saying this applies as well to the attitudes and opinions of the religious community no less than it does to the nation and its leaders.

This may be difficult, especially when it involves the refusal to fulfill what those others regard as "patriotic duty" binding upon all. The explicit recommendation of Vatican II that governments respect the rights of those whose commitment to peace obliges them to refuse to bear arms should be assured. If this recommendation is ignored, Christians, and especially Catholics, have the obligation to try to bring about the necessary changes. Although this nation does make provision for recognizing conscientious objection, that provision falls short of meeting the test and in a manner that should be of particular concern to Catholics. Selective Service law and regulations do not permit "selective conscientious objection," requiring instead an absolute rejection of "war in any form." In this it excludes those Catholics who adhere to the traditional theory which distinguishes between "just" and "unjust" war. Framed, as it was, to fit the pacifist commitment of the so-called "peace" churches (Society of Friends, Mennonites, Brethren, etc.) this amounts, in effect, to at least an implied violation of the constitutional protection against the preferential treatment of one set of religious beliefs over others. In a broader and more appropriate sense, of course, it violates the rights of anyone, Christian or not, whose refusal to participate in war is based on a personal conviction that it would violate his private conscience to do so.

The whole issue of conscientious objection deserves far more attention than it has received to this point. One is encouraged by advances made since this article was first published. A series of episcopal statements — crowned, of course, by the bishops' 1983 pastoral letter — have recognized the legitimacy of the stand for Catholics. In the blessedly brief Gulf War, in fact, there were some bishops who advised the faithful to consider becoming conscientious objectors if they were called to service and reminded those not subject to call of their obligation to honor and respect those who did.

There is still more to be done. Every Catholic pastor should take it upon himself to meet with local draft-board officials to clarify the bases for such objection to make certain that the young men who come before them (women, to this point at least, are not subject to registration or conscription) receive the fair and respectful hearing they have a right to expect.

The young Catholic whose conscience impels him to refuse military training and service (or who, after undergoing what the military calls "a crystallization of conscience," seeks discharge from the armed forces) is prepared to expect less than complete understanding and approval from secular authorities. More troubling is encountering the same lack of understanding and approval from his fellow Catholics and ecclesiastical superiors. This is where the "formation of conscience" is sadly at fault. A recently-completed study has revealed a shocking lack of coverage of the morality of war and conscientious objection in our Catholic high school religious studies programs. Not only should this be corrected without delay, but every Catholic parish should set up some kind of inquiry class — for adults as well as for children — to explore the issues that have been ignored for far too long.

If everyone agreed that the Christian vocation of peace requires total rejection of war and violence, would this not mean that nations in which Christians are numerous or even in the majority will be at a fatal disadvantage in a world where power relationships among nations ultimately rest upon the capacity and the readiness to wage war? It probably would.

This carries two crucial implications. The first is that steps should be taken now to prepare the Christian community (and those who might have to share its fate) to withstand the hardships it might suffer and seek ways of converting those hardships into occasions of grace. The defeat or destruction of nations is nothing new in human history; and to the believing Christian this is less of a catastrophe than preservation by immoral means. Accustomed to "the long view," Christians, if properly prepared, should be able to preserve their faith for future generations even if the "Christian West" were to collapse before its enemies. Ultimately, we know, the Gates of Hell will not prevail.

But there is no need to resign ourselves to so grim a fate. Part of the Christian mission of bringing peace to the world is to seek and find — *create*, if need be — moral and effective alternatives to war. First, and most obvious, is the replacing of the current system in which sovereign states pursue their own selfish interest, cooperating only to the extent those interests are enhanced or preserved by such cooperation, with an international body capable of establishing and maintaining order and authority. The United Nations as we know it today is at best a faint and most imperfect shadow of the type of world organization that is needed, but it has shown occasional flashes of promise enough to justify attempts to improve and ultimately perfect it.

Some beginnings have been made, most obvious the periodic worldwide emergency actions to lessen the impact of famine and other catastrophes. As Americans we can take pride, too, in the massive funds contributed through personal charity and governmental programs to a wide range of "foreign-aid" projects. It could be part of the Christian vocation for peace to go beyond this to promote and assist in the redistribution of world resources contemplated in the series of papal encyclicals beginning with *Rerum novarum* whose 100th anniversary was observed in 1991.

This will not be easy. Almost a quarter century has passed since I taught courses in Papal Social Encyclicals in a Catholic university and learned how little these documents stirred the hearts of even our more sensitive and well-intentioned young Catholics. Things may have changed here too, but I suspect (assuming the course is still taught) the students are no more prepared to accept any step which might seriously endanger the luxury standards of living we now enjoy. But that, I fear, is essential. The search for lasting world peace must include making every locality, every parish unit, a center of international concern and dedication to the well-being of all human beings. This does not mean returning to the old "foreign mission" emphasis upon playing the bountiful giver to those have have not "made the grade" and are not likely to. The key to world peace requires but must go further than charity and uplift; it lies instead in justice and a preferential option for the poor.

As a pacifist, I make no claim to having the whole answer to our problems of war and peace; but I'm fairly sure of the indispensable core and center of the answer: a total and unequivocal rejection of war and violence directed against my fellow humans, even (perhaps especially!) the brother who mistakenly sees in me his enemy. Once we get that far, once we exclude options that can no longer be (and probably never could be) reconciled with Christianity, we will be in a better position to explore the broader possibilities for achieving the more positive aspects of the Christian vocation for peace.

2. The Church and the Arms Race

The Vatican's 1976 statement to the UN on disarmament denounced the arms race as "a danger," "an injustice," "a form of theft," "a folly" and "a machine gone mad." "Even when they are not used," the statement charged, "by their cost alone armaments kill the poor by causing them to starve." The situation has worsened over the intervening years — the weapons more inhuman in their technology and killing power, their number vastly increased, and all countries, including the poorer, more heavily burdened with their cost. There have been other papal protests and statements since then, but they have had little effect. The UN has done no better in limiting or controlling the activities of the "merchants of death." As for the United States, it is — to our shame! — one of the leading suppliers of lethal power by sale and, often enough, by outright gift to "friendly" nations. When, as sometimes happens, that "friendship" wanes the deal backfires in embarrassing and very dangerous ways.

The collapse of the Soviet power bloc in East Europe raised hope for a time that the pattern might change. The anticipated "peace dividend" promised to shift the extravagant funds devoted to "defense" to more desperately needed domestic programs. The Persian Gulf war changed that, however, not only because of a perceived need to replace the armaments expended in battle but by opening vast new prospects of weapons modernization for our Middle Eastern "friends" under the guise of "promoting regional stability." One reads of a Congressional research report [Boston *Globe*, May 6, 1991] that this nation supplied more than $163.2 billion worth of military equipment to Middle East nations over a 14-year period (with the largest amount — $52.8 billion! — supplied to Iraq under our "friend" Saddam Hussein). Such "stability" should give one pause.

With the weaponry now at hand providing the potential to destroy the whole world and its inhabitants several times over, this insatiable drive to design, manufacture, and distribute new instruments capable of killing more people faster should be recognized and condemned as a diabolical distortion of right order. The heart of the problem is not theological but sociological. It is not that the Christian message has not been repeated over and over; rather, it has gone unheard or, if heard, ignored. That Vatican statement may have been the most explicit condemnation of war and violence issued in modern times, but there were few to listen or accept its implications. Ask the men and women in the pews — and I fear this would be true of many priests and bishops too — to identify the source of the papal denunciation, and most would shrug them off as the rantings of "peacenik" fanatics and let it go at that.

This article was first written in 1978, eleven years after Pope Paul VI designated January 1 as a "Day of Peace" to be observed annually "as a hope and a promise, at the beginning of the calendar which measures and outlines the path of human life in time, that peace with its just and beneficent equilibrium may dominate the events to come." Year after year, to the end of his reign, that same note was sounded from the Chair of Peter, and the practice has been followed by his successors. Paul's hope and promise have not been fulfilled.

Deservedly honored as the "Pilgrim of Peace" for breaking with Vatican tradition and travelling to different continents to deliver his message, he set the pattern that is followed today by John Paul II. One of those journeys brought him to the United States to challenge the UN with his dramatic appeal, "No more war! War never again!" Though his contributions — and certainly his travels — may have been overshadowed by the present Holy Father, they should not be allowed to vanish into the obscurity that has buried the life and works of that earlier "peace" pope, Benedict XV.

The Day of Peace messages, in particular, deserve attention as variations on the single major theme of peace, with each year giving emphasis to a particular aspect. In 1969 it was "Where there is no peace, right loses its human stature." [because] "Peace and rights are reciprocally the cause and effect of one another. Peace favors rights, and rights, in their turn, favor peace." In 1970 he zeroed in on the arms race, and what he said then has become an even greater shame for us today. "Lord, it is true: we are not on the right path. . . we have based the development of many of our giant industries on the diabolical capacity to produce arms of every size and shape, all designed to slaughter and exterminate men who are our brothers; thus we have cruelly established the economic stability of so many powerful nations upon the trading of arms to poor nations which lack ploughs, schools, and hospitals."

Subsequent messages focus more on individual potential and responsibility. In 1971 he chose as his theme "Peace is the product of love," in which he promised that "Whoever implants in public opinion the sentiment of human brotherhood without any limits, is preparing better days for the world." Papal statements of that day (now too?) may have been regrettably lacking in concern for sexually inclusive language, but this failing does not diminish their validity on that account. The following year he elaborated on what he meant by the "authentic notion of peace," tracing its source to "the sincere feeling for man." "A peace that does not well up from the true veneration of man is not peace in truth."

Each year added its lesson. The 1973 and 1974 messages were optimistic in tone, but an optimism with a sharp hook. "Peace is possible if it is truly desired. If peace is possible, it is a duty." With the war raging in Vietnam he seemed to recognize that many would dismiss that as a superficial piety and expanded upon the thought in more precise terms. "Let us not allow the idea of peace to perish, nor the hope for it, nor the aspiration toward it. . . . When peace has been cast out, let us open the door to it through honest negotiation brought to a sincere, positive conclusion."

That plea having been ignored for another year, he returned to it the next with an explicit rejection of the popular belief (and, alas, popular sociological theory) that conflict is a structural need of society. ". . . if public opinion has become a determining factor in the destiny of nations and people, then the fate of peace also depends on each one of us. . . . The point we wish to make is this: peace is possible if each of us wants it. Peace is possible if each of us cherishes it, if each of us fashions and develops a mentality oriented toward it, if each of us defends and works for peace. Each of us must heed the call of duty in our own conscience: peace depends on you too."

And so it goes. A single theme, an annual variation. One senses a growing intensity, each year's message more insistent. The year 1975 found Paul stressing reconciliation as the way to peace with special emphasis upon peace education which, he acknowledged, was no small or easy task. "Many, indeed very many problems are still susceptible of new solutions; the problems of yesterday are still with us; today will bring its own; tomorrow still others. But the solutions, we maintain, cannot and must never again issue from violent selfish conflict, much less from murderous wars among men."

And always, even when not explicitly addressed, the evil of the arms race is there as a concern. The 1976 message made it something of a carry-over from that 1975 conclusion: "Arms and wars must be excluded from any civilized approach to reality." Of special interest to Americans should have been the direct reference in that bicentennial year of an enduring blot upon our nation's history.

"If the consciousness of universal brotherhood really permeated the hearts of men, will they any longer need to arm themselves and become blind, fanatical murderers of their innocent brothers or, in the name of peace, to wreak destruction of unimaginable magnitude as at Hiroshima, August 6, 1945?" Nor is that all. As if to put in the sharpest context possible his denunciation of an act for which we bear the sole responsibility, he went on to praise Gandhi, "a single, frail man, armed only with the principle of nonviolence."

The year 1977 introduced the linkage upon which is based what is now termed "the seamless garment" in its theme, "Do we want peace? Then let us defend life." Hiroshima enters again as "terribly eloquent proof and a frighteningly prophetic example" of the catastrophe that looms on the horizon for the future if, in defiance of logic, humanity continues to ignore the inseparable nature of these two "supreme values in the civil order." Paul repeats the now familiar denunciation of the "false and dangerous program of the arms race" but here not only because of the threat of war it represents but, instead, as a reversal of what should be the Christian's priorities: "How can we fail to lament the incalculable outpourings of economic resources and human energies expended in order to preserve for each individual State its shield of ever more costly, ever more efficient, weapons; and this to the detriment of resources for schools, culture, agriculture, health and civic welfare?"

"No to violence; yes to peace!" That message had been repeated and repeated so many times that one suspects the Pope had reason to fear that the repetition itself might become counter-productive. Ten years before — during his trip to Bogota in August 1968 — he had made the point: "We must say and re-affirm that violence is not in accord with the Gospel; that it is not Christian."

So it went, year after year; and so it goes with John Paul II continuing the "Day of Peace" commemoration. The successor may not always keep to Paul's central theme, but the thrust is the same. Meanwhile the arms race goes on unabated. "Peace with its just and beneficent equilibrium" may receive more attention than it did then, but it cannot be said to "dominate the development of events" even in the Church in whose name those messages were addressed. We are still "not on the right path" — if anything, if the technological horrors of the Gulf War are considered, we have strayed farther away.

To the sociologist of religion the issue reduces itself to defining the proper relationship between religion and the social milieu and the need to create more effective means of communication between the two. All social institutions, religion included, must establish and maintain their respective positions within the society in which they exist and function — and in particular with the State, the institution of public authority, which, in modern times at least, has assumed the position of dominance.

It was not always so, of course. At earlier stages in history, the Family could claim priority; at certain times and places, Religion. Today, the power distribution is complicated by Religion's insistence upon priority for its values and the behavioral obligations those values might impose upon the believer who is also the citizen subject to the State and the behavioral obligations its values would impose. The complication reaches the critical point when the two appear to conflict. Ordinarily it is to the benefit of all the lesser institutions to establish a mutually supportive relationship with the State; but Religion's claim to a supernatural source and mission requires that it be ready at times to "stand in judgment" when the demands of secular authority threaten or undermine the higher values entrusted to it.

This, of course, is where the "prophetic function" of which we so often speak (but, alas, are not always eager to recognize and embrace in actual practice) becomes relevant. The problem of the Church and the arms race and, beyond that, the vision of peace Paul presents requires a more active and effective exercise of that function. Not to actively oppose the ever-escalating commitment to new and more efficient instruments of slaughter is to betray the sacred mission the Church and its members profess to serve.

Of course, it is never easy to move against the stream; and it is especially difficult, not to say dangerous, to take on the State. The danger of reprisal, even persecution, can tempt spiritual leaders to moderate their protests lest they put "too great a burden" upon the followers. For their part, the faithful faced with a call to moral resistance will exploit loopholes and ambiguities in picking those elements of that call which are least threatening or inconvenient to them. Taking Pope Paul's annual appeals as an example, measuring the directness of his message against the weakness of the response, it becomes evident that there is a serious failure of communication to be overcome. In isolation the variations on the theme hide its consistency, but to study the texts in fuller presentation and detail is to risk losing both theme and consistency in the etiquette of papal style and prudence.

When it comes to issues touching upon what states define as their national interests and security interests in particular, modern popes, speaking as responsible spokesmen for the Church Universal, shy away from pointing the finger or naming names. It is because it was so great a departure from usual papal rhetoric that Paul's explicit reference to Hiroshima comes as something of a shock, but it is important to note that he does not make equally explicit reference by name to the nation that wreaked the unimaginable destruction of which he spoke (elsewhere translated as "butchery of untold magnitude") or to the responsibility of the Catholic citizens of that nation, *including those directly involved in dropping the bomb*. Not only that, shocking though the statement may be in both milder and tougher versions, one should not overlook that even this departure from the papal style and practice came thirty years and more after the tragic fact.

There is always the problem, too, that papal statements (episcopal pastorals as well, though there has been improvement here) must be couched in, if not smothered by, scriptural and theological references and pious exhortations. There may be no way of avoiding this completely since, if the case is to be made, it must be made in religious/moral terms. However, the statements would have greater impact if more of an effort were made to spell things out in terms more familiar to the believer who is expected to guide his behavior according to what is said and keep ecclesiastical embellishments to the unavoidable minimum. There is much to be said for "telling it like it is" when it comes to something as important as war and peace so that those to whom the message is directed will not dismiss what is said as something not really relevant to them but just another exercise in spiritual platitudes and formal pieties. Pius XII, let us remember, did protest injustices done to "alien" population groups; unfortunately, he never openly protested what the German government was doing to the Jews, native as well as alien.

If the position of the Church regarding the arms race and its attendant evils is to reach the broader Catholic public and, through its influence, have an effect upon national and international policy, it must be given special and exclusive attention. For the most part, Paul VI met that test. It should also provide leads to what and how that influence can be employed. There, I fear, his otherwise remarkable Peace Day messages fell short.

The linkage of peace with the abortion issue ("Do you want peace? Then let us defend life!") illustrates this. There is no doubt as to where the Catholic Church stands with respect to abortion or of its readiness to oppose every assault, real or imagined, against that "right to life" issue. Would it not be possible to promote equally intensive and effective opposition to the arms race which, in its way, is equally if not potentially more destructive of human life? Could not an equally dedicated network of parish and other affiliated organizations be marshaled against nuclear and neutron bombs or for the conversion of the nation's resources to the service of its social needs and away from the production of state-of-the-art instruments for the wholesale destruction of human life?

"Peace is possible if it is truly wanted. If peace is possible, it is a duty." Unfortunately even the strongest statements by religious leaders in support of peace and disarmament are weakened, sometimes rendered pragmatically meaningless, by the intrusion of "prudent qualifications" which are seized upon by the hearer as a justification for continuing just as before. If our "no to violence" and "yes to peace" are to carry any weight, there must be no doubt whatever about the firmness and sincerity of the speaker's total commitment to them. If "violence is not in accord with the Gospel and cannot be Christian" this should mean that war, the ultimate form of violence, cannot ever be justified; that the Church as social institution and as moral community created to uphold and give witness to the Christian truth can never encourage, support, approve, or condone war in general or any war in particular.

Communication lives not in words alone. It should be a matter of grave concern, then, if the Church or its agencies by their actions confuse or even seem to contradict the message they should be proclaiming. If it would be a scandal for a Catholic medical school to train its students in the techniques of abortion, it should be no less so for a college or university to provide training in the arts of war. What good does it do for a pope to declare that "arms and wars must be excluded from any civilized approach to reality" when a major segment of the nations' armed forces (estimated at one-third or more) are Catholics and many of their officers products of military programs conducted under Catholic college auspices? Given Paul VI's unfavorable characterization of "giant industries" which profit from "the diabolical capacity to produce arms of every size and shape, all designed to slaughter and exterminate men who are our brothers," is it really appropriate for a Catholic university to boast of having contributed some discovery essential to the making of the nuclear bomb or to develop and help recruit agents for the C.I.A.? Is it proper for bishops to be silent about those same "giant industries" located in their dioceses and staffed by their parishioners? Or to invest parish or diocesan funds in government securities which support or in industries which profit from the merchandising of death?

If complete separation from involvement in these things is asking too much, there are other steps to be considered. Efforts should be made to counteract the influences of war and the arms race. Parishes and Catholic schools should become centers of peace teaching and activity. Dioceses might adopt the practice followed in some European countries and set aside one Sunday each year for special collections to fund organizations and programs devoted to peace and disarmament. Instead of military displays and memorials, churches should give prominence to the peace witnesses and martyrs of its earliest days and due honor to those of its members who reject and refuse to cooperate with agencies of militarization and war.

The annual commemoration of the World Day of Peace must become more than an empty ritual. Surely this was not what Paul VI intended it to be. In the prayer he composed on the occasion of the first commemoration he appealed to the "God of Peace" to "Open our minds and hearts ever wider to the real demands of the love of all our brothers, so that we may more completely become peacemakers."

That prayer has not yet been answered, and we have not yet found that "right path" of which he spoke. But we can at least take some comfort in knowing gains have been made and more will be made if each of us, in his or her own way, does everything in our power to bring the nation and our Church closer to the goal by making every day a day in which to say "no" to violence and "yes" to peace. Peace is possible if we really want it; we have Paul's assurance on that. But as he spelled it out almost two decades ago, "Each of us must heed the call of duty in his own conscience. Peace depends on you, too."

3.

Catholic Opposition to Hitler: The Perils of Ambiguity

In their introduction to *Religion and Society in Tension*, Charles Y. Glock and Rodney Stark make the point that, at least in Judeo-Christian cultures, "religion is expected to be at odds with the world around it." If this is a normal state of affairs, how much more intense the strain and antagonisms must be in a "world" dominated by a state authority openly dedicated to the objective of subverting organized religion to serve its own purposes or, if that is not possible, eliminating it and its influence altogether. Since the emergence of such states seems to be a recurring event in the history of man, a definite sociological problem presents itself as to how the religious community is to cope with them. Adolf Hitler's Third Reich is deserving of special mention if only in that it is among the most recent and more successful of such attempts.

One might be tempted to balk at the "Judeo-Christian culture" description in the context of the Nazi experience, but the fact is that throughout its aborted "thousand year" reign, the National Socialist regime continued to present itself to supporters, admirers, and opponents alike as "the defender of Western Civilization." Even its efforts to expunge the "Judeo" component of that Western heritage (and, in the process, exterminate its living representatives) were justified, assuming that word can be used in this connection, in terms of perfecting and purifying the culture stream Germany shared and still shares with the other nations of "the Christian West."

The problem of dealing with the Christian Churches was somewhat more complicated. The ultimate goal may have been the same, the complete eradication of Christianity — though in fairness one might question whether this was actually the goal for any but the more extremist Party ideologues. In any event, even for these, it had to be a dream deferred. This did not mean, of course, that the churches had to be tolerated until such time as the regime was ready and able to give them the full treatment; instead, there was a gradual acceleration and intensification of the struggle as the totalitarian power succeeded in consolidating itself. For many different reasons, this particular struggle reached something of a peak in relations between the Nazi state and the Roman Catholic Church and its imposing network of auxiliary organizations. And it was a two-sided struggle, though a losing and finally hopeless one for the church. The only notable exception to the string of defeats that began with liquidation of church-related organizations, the deconfessionalization of the schools, the formal restriction of religious services and activities, and, ultimately, the dissolution of convents and religious orders was the "victory" won by the Church on the euthanasia issue.

Historians of the Nazi era have provided us with a generously documented record of the struggle. It shows that the principal explanation of why the battles ended in defeat lay, first, in the greater range of effective force available to the secular power and, second, in the failure of the leaders of the religious community to inspire the kind of resistance that might have brought Hitler to his Canossa. Hidden behind this explanation, however, is a more troubling suggestion that these religious leaders never really thought the outcome could be otherwise, that from the very beginning they operated on the prudential (and probably correct) assumption that if they were to risk issuing a call to spiritual arms against the state, their "troops" probably would not have rallied to the cause.

The implications of this for the sociologist of religion should be obvious. An assumption of a lack of commitment, which is really what this posture of prudent self-restraint reflected, must effectively undermine the essential viability of the church association as an institutional structure. At the very least it destroys the basis for any significantly prophetic function (the "sacred mission to denounce and resist matters of the flesh," as Glock and Stark have it). The thesis to be set forth and illustrated in this highly exploratory paper is that such was the case for the German Catholic Church under the Nazi tyranny. Lest this be misunderstood, it should be added at once that there is no intent to deny the truly heroic resistance mounted by individual spokesmen and members of the Catholic Church or to dishonor the sacrifices, even of life, they made for their religious faith.

As indicated this is an exploration and will probably seem to be lacking in scientific quality as that term has come to be defined. In a sense we are limited to such tentative and admittedly impressionistic efforts if only because such data as are available are too spotty and much too inconclusive to support a more thorough and systematic analysis. Nor is it possible to test the validity of the reflective commentary to be offered here. Cogent though these observations may appear, a quite contrary and equally persuasive interpretation could be proposed by others.

Early in 1970 a pastor in a small Bavarian village wrote to ask whether I might be interested in seeing the accumulation of diocesan instructions and notices his predecessor had saved during the Nazi years. The eager anticipation with which I answered his inquiry faded considerably when the package finally arrived: most of the items were for the pre-war years, and virtually all of them had already been published in one documentary collection or another. Nevertheless, included among the almost 140 items were two which, treated as a unit, provide dramatic illustrations of the strength and the weakness of the Church's efforts to protest and oppose the repressive measures directed against it.

On 31 January 1937, the Reverend Johannes Kraus, rector of the Eichstaett Cathedral parish, mounted his pulpit and delivered a scathing denunciation of false and scandalous reports in the local press which, he felt, were aimed at discrediting and vilifying the Catholic priesthood. On 12 April of that same year, Bishop Michael Rackl of Eichstaett used the same forum to announce and denounce police orders that had been issued to Kraus giving him twenty-four hours to leave the diocese. Two sermons can not tell the whole story of the church-state struggle, not even in that single diocese, but they give clear evidence of what proved to be an unquestionably effective and, at the same time, eminently self-defeating line of defense.

Dompfarrer Kraus was straightforward enough. Declaring that his sole objective was to counteract the smear campaign being waged against the priesthood and promising to speak not an uncharitable word, he quickly moved to a general statement in the abstract of the theme that he was to personalize in the body of his remarks. Catholics in Germany were compared with the "ancient Israelites" (in retrospect, perhaps not the happiest of identifications to choose, but this was before the anti-Jewish campaign reached full momentum): "We returned from the Great War with our other fellow citizens; we all suffered alike the inflation and the years of crisis; we felt and saw the wounds from which our people were bleeding; we endured the effects of the lost war and we wanted to build, nothing more than to build." But time and again, Catholics found their efforts disrupted so that "it became necessary to leave the workplace and take up defense." In the single year he had served as their pastor, he had been obliged to rise to such defense on two previous occasions,[1] but these had brought him little notice or opposition until he dared to take public issue with the controlled press and its anti-Catholic propaganda.

Three items in particular were to be reviewed: (1) an openly anti-Semitic letter to the notorious *Stuermer* by a writer who identified himself as a priest; (2) the great wave of publicity given the case of a

[1]The first had to do with leaflets and placards distributed by opponents of the confessional schools; the second a public defense of Archbishop Groeber of Freiburg after that dignitary had been attacked at a gathering in the vicinity.

seventeen-year-old "theology student" charged with sexual perversion; and (3) a journalistic account of a visit to Dachau in which the author described a "chance" meeting with an internee (also a sex deviant) identified as a priest who had formerly served in Rome as a secret negotiator between the Vatican and Moscow. Each item in term was systematically and factually refuted in the Kraus sermon: no official directory carried a priest by the name signed to the *Stuermer* letter; the unfortunate young man was a high school student who, whatever his career aspirations might have been, could neither have been engaged in nor accepted for priestly studies; and, when pressed for more explicit facts, the journalist (apparently well-known for other anti-Catholic "feature" articles) came up with a quite different description of the man he had talked to at Dachau.

It was the second item, however, that served as the vehicle for the Kraus protest. The identification of this young man as a theology student and, by this device, extending his personal misdeeds to reflect upon the priesthood itself was as illogical and unjust, in Kraus's eyes, as would have been an attempt to smear the officer caste with those misdeeds had the young man expressed an interest in a military career instead. It was an effective logical argument, of course, but Kraus did not intend to stop with that. As a former officer, he found such an attempt an affront to his honor, and he would be bound to protest.

> I am an old front-line officer and have given of my heart's blood for the Fatherland. At the Somme I earned Saxony's Friedrich August medal; at Verdun, the Iron Cross; at Damenweg, the silver medal for bravery; in Aillywald, the Order of Bavaria with crown and swords; and in the battle of Amiens in 1918, the Iron Cross, first class. My left arm was wounded by a grenade splinter, my right upper arm bored by a machine-gun bullet so that even today I do not have full strength in it; my right lung was pierced, and I have undergone three operations as an aftermath of this. Two of my ribs

were broken. I have gone through the strongest crossfire without falling back. In the advances I scorned cover. When I went forward the soldiers followed me blindly because they considered me invulnerable — and all of my regimental comrades, with whom I am still bound in the true brotherhood of arms, would testify to this.

Having made his point in the context of the hypothetical case, he then drove the argument home in the actual case at hand. "And now I should forget honor, meekly accept the blows on my head which are raining down upon clergy who served in the war as much as upon the others priests and the Church herself — and from those who were still in swaddling clothes when we were shedding our blood for the Fatherland?"

The argument did not end with this, however. The litany of personal war sacrifices was also linked to his refusal to contribute to the various "voluntary" collections organized by the Nazi state. It was not, he assured his listeners, a matter of refusing help to those who needed it (he gave his contributions to the Catholic charities) but, rather, symbolic protest against violations of rights and privileges supposedly guaranteed by the Concordat between the Vatican and the Third Reich. He felt secure in taking such a position, he went on, because he need never "fear the charge that I do not love the Fatherland." As he put it, "I have proven my love for the Fatherland; I prove it every day as one of Christ's officers when, in keeping with the words of the dying Field Marshal von Hindenburg, I see to it that Christ is preached in Germany."

The reference to the revered military leader and former President is reflected and expanded in the crescendo of patriotic fervor which brings the sermon to its end: "Everything for Germany, and Germany for Christ! And again: Everything for Germany, and Germany for Christ! And yet a third time the pledge: Everything for Germany, and Germany for Christ!"

Surely a tough act to follow, but less than three months later Bishop Rackl proved more than equal to the task. Here we have the added benefit of parenthetical insertions at appropriate points in the mimeographed text describing the hearers' reactions to his remarks. These include no less than ten references to applause (ranging from "long" or "sustained" to "loud," "stormy," and in one instance "tumultuous") and two references to jeers and whistles of derision directed against actions or statements attributed to the Church's opponents by the bishop.

He began by summarizing the situation: the suddenness of the order requiring their pastor to leave the diocese; the failure to provide specific charges or follow procedural formalities; the bishop's own response in the form of telegraphed protests and appeals for assistance to Hitler and all other concerned officials along with instructions not to leave his assigned post (an announcement which brought the first outburst of "stormy" applause). He then addressed himself to the broader meaning of the action, prefacing his remarks on this subject with a disclaimer of any intent to stir passions which might not be fully compatible with the Christian ideal of love.

That out of the way, he launched into a statement of his case couched in the most passionately nationalistic terms. He spoke of the cruelty of driving from his native province a dedicated priest who had "poured out his heart's blood" in the nation's battles, particularly at a time when the nation had "learned anew to understand the meaning of soldierly honor and officer's honor" a "healthy" understanding, in his eyes, that was never completely lost to the German people, not even in "the dark days" of the 1918 Revolution. Referring with approval to the ceremonial honor paid to the Unknown Soldier, he reminded his audience that respect and memorials were due the "known" soldiers as well (wild applause). In what must have been a particularly telling thrust, he voiced his "deepest pain" that the authorities had chosen to treat this former officer in a manner usually reserved for dealing with a pimp.

A reference in that morning's newspaper to "circles in Eichstaett who think they can march against the State" is characterized by Rackl as "today's declaration of war" and used as the opportunity to move full steam ahead on the patriotism theme:

> I take it this is supposed to mean in particular that the *Dompfarrer* belongs to those who march against the State. (stormy cries of "pfui") My friends! once again I say: anyone who has stood at the Front for four long years, at the very frontmost lines for Germany's honor and well-being, has never marched against the State and can not march against the State. (loud applause) And once an officer of the Fatherland has become in addition an officer of the Catholic Church, an officer of Jesus Christ, an officer of God — then that Loyalty which is inscribed on his banner is a Loyalty toward State and Fatherland as well. No one loves his Fatherland more truly than the Catholic priest.

That rousing affirmation was extended at once to the full range of issues troubling church-state relations. The bishop mentioned his own experiences with threatening crowds outside his palace; the injustices and indignities suffered by the Church in all spheres of activity; the denial of the opportunity and the right, even in the religious press, to answer and refute the scurrilous charges and rumors directed against the Church and her priests. As he saw it, a new *Kulturkampf* was under way, with the important difference being that where Bismarck had tried to win the people away from the Church, his Nazi successors were moving systematically to isolate the priests from people. It was, therefore, a time to renew one's loyalty to the Church and its priesthood and to pray for grace and strength from above.

> I believe the State knows the *Dompfarrer* is no revolutionary! (applause) The struggle is between two ideologies

> which are as opposed to each other as fire is opposed to water. And in the struggle the Church now sees what a dangerous opponent she has in the State! We have always been loyal and wish to be obedient to the State unto death. (loud applause) But one thing we will never permit any power on earth to take from us: our holy Catholic faith! (shouts "never," "never")

Affirming once again that "in our love and in our loyalty to the German Fatherland and in our love and loyalty to the holy Catholic Church we will never allow others to surpass us," he concluded with a call for a "crusade of prayer" and dedicated the first prayer to "our German Fatherland . . . that the sun of peace may shine over the German provinces of our truly and deeply beloved German homeland."

What we have in these two sermons — and it is a pattern to be found in whatever formal and public Catholic opposition to Hitler did exist — is a combination of strong, explicit protest and equally strong affirmations of patriotism and national loyalty. In its historical context, the protest was truly heroic both in its clarity and its directness. The very fact that it led to official reprisals such as that taken against Kraus is testimony to its effectiveness. It might be noted in passing that while Bishop Rackl did not suffer the same consequences for this or his other pronouncements of similar content,[1] his colleague, Bishop Sproll of Rottenburg, was not so fortunate. Sproll, like Kraus, was formally exiled and, in fact, removed bodily from his diocese, the only German Catholic bishop to receive so serious a penalty from the Nazi regime. Whatever legitimate criticism one may make of the Christian churches for their failure to produce an adequate witness for that unhappy time, it must be said to their credit that, weak and unsuccessful though it may have been, they

[1] An equally emotional sermon — once again protesting the exile of another of his priests — was preached by Rackl at Ochsenfurt some weeks later.

represented the only institutional source of open and public opposition to the tyranny.

The emphasis placed on the other element, the patriotic motif, was equally open and public and at least as strong. At times, indeed, its superheated emotional tone boiled over into nothing less than rabble-rousing nationalism. The Kraus-Rackl sermons, as the audience reaction inserts make quite clear, reached several such peaks of enthusiasm. What we have, then, given the peculiarities of the situation, is a pairing of two not altogether compatible themes, an exercise in studied ambiguity. It was, needless to say, a tactical ambiguity in that it represented an attempt to set the protest in the form most likely to evoke the desired response from the listening faithful and still, if possible, avoid penalty or suppression. Since the German Catholic was just as much exposed and just as vulnerable to the ultra-nationalistic milieu created by the architects of the Third Reich as were their fellow citizens, the language of patriotic commitment may have been the only vehicle to assure any kind of hearing. This seems, at least, to have been the judgment of the official spokesmen of the Church.

To this extent the stress placed upon the battlefield sacrifices of a Kraus, together with the indignant rejection of any suggestion of disloyalty on his part, must be seen as a calculated rhetorical device. It would be much too simple, however — and probably an insult to the churchmen who used this device — to assume that this was all it was. The national pride, the patriotic fervor, and, it would even more certainly follow, the indignation voiced in these sermons were unquestionably real and sincere. It scarcely bears noting that this would be equally true of the enthusiastic echo their words found in the heart of the listener in the pew.

There is no way to determine the actual impact of these patriotic effusions.That they were singularly ineffective in convincing the Nazis is clear enough from the pattern of continued and intensified persecution. Of course, this in itself proves little: it is quite possible that without this fervent and public exploitation of wartime heroism as evidence of Catholic loyalty, the pace of the persecution might have been speedier and the defeat of the church much more complete.

In our readiness to make this allowance, however, we must not disregard other equally important effects that appeals of this nature would almost certainly produce. In a situation of crisis in which the tension between church and state is heightened to the danger point, ambiguity, whatever tactical justification it may possess, has its perils as well. At the very least it can operate to confuse and blur the very issues it is to the interest of the religious community to define as sharply as possible. In the present case, for instance, the Nazi authorities and their captive press had embarked upon a deliberate campaign to undercut the influence of the Catholic Church and its leadership by drastically restricting their sphere of permissible activities and attempting to destroy their public image. Kraus made specific reference to this: "Children point their fingers at us and their elders murmur among themselves, 'There's another one of those.' You all know what I mean." Then, when someone like Kraus did dare to respond to these attacks and speak out in defense of the priesthood, he was simply removed from the scene by arbitrary police action. This was the issue, but the rhetoric of the sermons converted it into something else. It now became a matter of denouncing these smears and unjust punitive actions *because they were directed against heroes who had fought and bled for Germany,* men who deserved better treatment from the nation and its rulers. The essential fact that priests *as priests* were being slandered — and that this was to be protested even if the victim had not so much as a day of military service to his credit — was simply smothered by this blanket of super-patriotic rhetoric.

Distortion of the real issues at stake is bad enough, but other more subtle effects must be recognized as perils too. That same flag-waving, bloody-shirt rhetoric which was intended to arouse the indignation of the hearers (and clearly did) could not fail to reinforce the Nazis' own efforts to instill and exploit nationalistic pride and identification in the hearts of the general public. In this way the religious opposition actually helped the regime to secure the foundations for the totalitarian power which would later be turned against the Church.

After listening to sermons like these, Catholics would emerge indignant; but it is at least equally certain that they would also emerge "charged up" in their emotional attachment to German national traditions and the patriotic virtues. Once the Catholic faithful were convinced that "no one loves his Fatherland more truly than the Catholic priest," the conclusions to be drawn concerning their own obligations to the nation's leaders should be obvious enough.

The contribution made by the patriotism component of the protest-and-patriotism tactic to the Nazi propaganda drive had still another effect that could only prove dysfunctional to the Church and its interests. The vast majority of the faithful, even assuming they might not be in full sympathy with the regime, were not, as the old phrase has it, "thirsting for martyrdom" or, for that matter, looking for any avoidable trouble with the authorities. Even making due allowance for the effects of selective perception, the German Catholic citizen would have to be extremely obtuse not to realize that his church was under severe pressure and extremely insensitive not to be worried by that fact.

Sermons like the two discussed here not only put the situation in distressingly clear perspective, but they usually included passages specifically calling for the kind of spiritual heroism that might endanger the comfortable patterns of compromise and conformity that most of the Catholic faithful had been able to achieve in their individual lives. If this were all, the citizen who was also a believer would have been faced with an unpleasant but inescapable choice. But it was not all. How helpful it must have been to find these troubling details of persecution and injustice interwoven with sentiments exhorting the faithful to loyalty and obedience to the state. "Everything for Germany and Germany for Christ" may have carried all sorts of subtle overtones for *Dompfarrer* Kraus that his listeners did not catch or, in what may have been the majority of cases, *would not have wanted to catch*. As a result, those very same qualities of ambiguity that, it was hoped, would mollify the Nazi authorities actually opened the way for the man in the pew to avoid drawing the intended conclusions.

In summary, then, the failure of the Catholic Church to mount an effective opposition to Hitler's Third Reich was due, at least in part, to this failure to "tell it like it was" and to insist that its members "stand up and be counted" against tyranny. How substantial a part this played in that failure is beyond our power at this point in time and space to determine. It may well be that a contrary course would have failed, too, with even more disastrous consequences.

This is admittedly an inconclusive note upon which to end this modest attempt to explore and interpret that record; but even if we are less than happy with the highly tentative answers we have suggested, at least there is some satisfaction in having focused attention upon questions that all too often have been ignored or overlooked in the literature dealing with the "struggle between Cross and Swastika."

There may be some important lessons to be learned as well for churches and their leaders who may in other times and places find themselves confronted with governments, whether professedly democratic or authoritarian, whose polices or programs represent a threat to the religious practices and teachings it is their responsibility to uphold and spread. In any such future tests — that is, whenever the tension between church and state becomes acute — it might be instructive to reflect upon the German experience before preferring the wisdom of serpents, represented by the kind of tactical ambiguity described here, over the direct simplicity of authentic prophetic witness. And if, as the Berrigans (brother-priests charged with complicity in a bombing-and-kidnap plot) and others might insist, such a crisis is upon us here and now, the lesson is particularly timely.

4.
Total War and "Absolute" Pacifism

For fifteen hundred years and more the major Christian communions have found it difficult, often impossible, to come to terms with what many see as inescapable pacifist implications of the faith they profess. Today the dilemma has been made more acute by developments in military technology as well as the emergence of nation/states which, at best, are religiously neutral but in situations of international strain or conflict inclined to resent any "intrusion" of moral considerations into questions of policy. It was an American Secretary of State, not the representative of the officially atheist Soviet Union, who declared his viewpoint on negotiating crises as follows: "The criteria should be hardheaded in the extreme. Decisions are not helped by considering them in terms of sharing, brotherly love, the Golden Rule, or inducting our citizens into the Kingdom of Heaven."

The disparity between such pragmatism and the attitudes and practices of "primitive" Christianity in the centuries closest to its Founder and His earliest disciples is immediately obvious. The authentic Christian commitment then was to nonviolence and to pacifism in an absolute sense. The English historian, Stanley Windass, has argued convincingly that the sense of being bound by the Gospel teachings of nonresistance to the evildoer, coupled with self-sacrificial love, even for the enemy, was not the product of an "aberrant stream of thought" but, instead, the *only* stream of thought. What some have advanced as evidence to the contrary — occasional and obscure references on Roman burial inscriptions, for instance — reflect individual behavior, not community practice. As such they prove nothing beyond what anyone familiar with the weaknesses of human nature might take for granted: then, as since, Christians have not always practiced what their Church preached.

The conversion of the Empire under Constantine brought a profound change, one which, as the preliminary draft of the American bishops' 1983 pastoral letter on war and peace proposed, made it "necessary" to consider under what conditions a believer might serve in the military. Though one might challenge the *necessity* of such a change in emphasis and direction, that it did take place cannot be denied. The appropriateness of St. Maximilian's witness ("I cannot serve as a soldier; I cannot do evil. I am a Christian.") was unlikely to be questioned by a persecuted minority which repeatedly witnessed "brothers and sisters in the Spirit" carried away, tortured and even torn apart by ravenous beasts for the entertainment of a howling mob. In time it would seem less appropriate when such refusal was directed against an Empire which was now protector and promoter of Christianity. Still, it would be wrong to reduce the history of the "Age of Martyrs" to a simple and circumstantial expression of political dissent. The unwillingness of Maximilian and others to violate their consciences found deeper wellsprings in the teachings and example of Christ himself.

As those earliest Christians saw it, the rejection of all violence had its source in Scriptural instructions and incidents — in the Sermon on the Mount with its Beatitudes; in the rebuke of Peter for his impulsive resort to the sword; above all, in the Passion and Crucifixion and the call to take up the Cross and follow Him. These defined a new order of obligation. The old "eye-for-an-eye" morality was overturned and replaced by readiness to forgive (seventy times seven times, if need be!). The Christian pacifism of succeeding generations unto our own continues in much the same vein, finding renewed confirmation in the models provided by Maximilian, Martin of Tours, and the multitude of martyrs and saints, known and unknown, who have given witness to the truth with their lives.

It is vital that we do not forget this history despite the theories and practices which have come to dominate the mainstream Christian churches in the post-Constantinian era. That original "stream of thought" still flows and has found expression in the words and witness of inspired individuals and perfection-seeking communities down the centuries. Sometimes these have been rejected as "heretic" and hunted down by the combined forces of Church and State. Since the Reformation they may have gained recognition (though not always toleration) as what we now call the "historic peace churches." Roman Catholicism, for its part, has found it convenient to make place in its roster of honored saints for believers who lived lives marked by total commitment and literal behavioral application of the Scriptural injunctions and counsels. On occasion, too, the continuity of Christian pacifism was preserved in the emergence of religious orders, the Franciscans being perhaps the most obvious example of this.

There is no denying, however, that such lingering adherence to pacifist tradition was overwhelmed by the acceptance and development of the concept of justifiable war introduced by St. Augustine and given more precise and sophisticated elaboration by St. Thomas and later Scholastics. The barbarians at the gates threatening the now converted Empire presented devout Christians with their first really crucial crisis of conscience. The simple and direct choice between mundane and eternal values was transformed into a choice between conflicting moral obligations, *both* of which were now invested with divine sanction. If too much has been made of the imperial oath as explanation of previous patterns of refusal, that concern was now negated by the declared obligation to obey legitimate authority in the person of a consecrated Christian prince. Spiritual functionaries (priests, bishops and other "holy people") were still expected, and later canonically obliged to remain aloof from the bloodshed and violence of war, but the ordinary Christian who could not claim such special status or calling would be subject to ridicule, ostracism, and worse if unwilling to perform the duties laid upon him.

The "just war" teachings were originally permissive and merely opened the way for the loyal Christian subject to serve in the military while still fulfilling his obligation as believer. It was an *exception* to the normal perspective on war which still implied the pacifism of the early Church. Unfortunately, but predictably, in practice if not in theory, this restrictive character of the "just war" formulation was generally ignored. In time, in fact, it was canceled out by the principle which held that, in case of doubt, the presumption of justice was to be made in favor of legitimate authority. In effect this would all but exclude the possibility of what the sociologist would describe as religiously motivated and approved deviance in time of war.

Theologians and moral philosophers in their insistence upon the immutability of natural and divine Law do not always welcome the intervention of the social scientist in areas over which they claim exclusive domain. Recent advances in scholarship, however, have made it clear that a deepened understanding of the situational, motivational, and behavioral dimensions of human actions have much to offer.

Certainly this is true with reference to the morality of war. Where the historian's work is essential to an awareness of the absurdities of the Crusades as shocking evidence of how far reversal of Christian values had gone in the past, the political analysis of the rise and nature of the nation/state can demonstrate how close we have come to making that reversal complete in our time.

After all, the Crusades, whatever else they may have been, were at least an expression of grotesquely distorted religious commitment. Contemporary wars on the other hand, despite the propagandist's skill in providing idealistic gloss to their objectives and assertions of divine approval and support, find their immediate (and ultimate) justification in the defense or acquisition of territory and resources and the infinitely expandable demands of "national security."

Since the notion of a "just" war logically implies the existence of an "unjust" war, it introduced the option of a limited or "selective" pacifism. If a war, to be justified, must meet certain carefully defined conditions, it should follow that any given war which does not must be denied the support and participation of the Christian. The scandal of witnessing the Mystical Body of Christ repeatedly torn apart as Christians fought on virtually every side of every war to come along suggests that logic did not always, or often, rule. To be even a theoretical option such "selective" pacifism would be limited to those few who possessed the intellectual and theological sophistication required. And even so gifted a minority would find themselves hamstrung by that further "principle" granting the presumption of justice to the war-making authorities in case of doubt.

Of course, those few who refused to go along were not obliged to make their refusal public. The failure to volunteer the expected measure of support for the cause might evoke criticism or even condemnation as a sign of selfishness, cowardice, or worse. Nevertheless, it was possible for the "selective" pacifist — should he or she so choose — to keep it a personal, and private, matter.

The advent of universal conscription, one of the crucial distinguishing characteristics of modern war, destroyed this possibility, at least for those made subject to military service. With conscription came a depersonalization of loyalty. Now it was no longer a sense of the volunteer warrior's attachment to the leader and his cause, or, if that were present, it was not essential. Devotion to a charismatic leader (Napoleon, Hitler, etc.) might enhance commitment to the abstraction of "the Fatherland" and its symbols, but it was that abstraction that held prior claim and had the power to enforce its demands upon the individual citizen.

Already between the first two world wars, a gathering of European theologians condemned Nationalism as "the characteristic heresy" of the day, a judgment that has been validated and confirmed many times ever since. A distinguished naval officer's sentiments expressed in a famous toast ("Our country, may she always be in the right; but our country, right or wrong.") may be forgiven as an innocent display of theological ignorance or insensitivity, but to have those sentiments publicly echoed by America's most prominent ecclesiastic in the context of the infamous war in Vietnam was a scandal of the highest order. No less shocking, and probably far more costly in its consequences, was the virtually unanimous record of active support for Hitler's wars on the part of German Christians and their spiritual leaders.

Few more glaring examples of the "heresy" of nationalism can be found than the wartime pastorals of Germany's *Feldbischof* Rarkowski. On the occasion of his 70th birthday, for example, he reminisced upon the rebirth of the military forces under Hitler as "a change for the better" and proceeded to praise the new era and its new young army "which under its *Fuehrer* and Supreme Commander has, since 1939, performed immortal deeds and reached the heights of accomplishment in offense and defense on all the battlefields of the present war."

Cardinal Francis Spellman, like Rarkowski, was designated bishop to the armed forces; but it would be a serious mistake to write such nationalistic excesses off as simply an occupational hazard. Though more restrained in expression, perhaps, similar sentiments were voiced by other bishops as well, not excluding some of the more heroic opponents of the Nazi regime. It is something of a cliche that political differences must stop "at the water's edge" or where other national boundaries set the patriotic limit. It is a betrayal of Christian universality if the same should prove true of the application of moral principles in time of war.

The second defining characteristic of modern war — linked to conscription as both cause and effect — is that it has become total in nature and scope. The contesting combatants are now entire populations. Uniformed warriors have become but one resource among many to be exploited or attacked, and increasingly this resource has diminished in importance. In theory and in practice the concept of a legitimate target of hostile action has been expanded to include all persons or activities capable of making a potential contribution, no matter how indirect, to the maintenance of the wartime economy or national morale.

In "total" war there are no noncombatants. The worker in the munitions factory; the farmer in his fields; the teacher in the classroom teaching the virtues of loyal citizenship; the housewife saving fats and cans; even the grade school children contributing pennies towards the purchase of a bomb — all become targets for destruction by weapons specifically designed to destroy them. Is the day-care center which frees mothers for work in the armaments factory not as legitimate a target as the factory itself? In the logic of total war, the answer is obvious. Ironically enough, even the pacifist is locked into the logic of total war: by refusing to pay taxes because they make him guilty of participating in the destruction and killing he deplores, does he not pass that same judgment upon his counterpart on the other side who fails to make the same refusal?

The reality of total war, in short, has reduced the "just war" teaching and tradition to a pious fiction. Some, of course, might insist it never was anything more, but now at least the truth is there for all to see and acknowledge. Even "limited" wars — witness Vietnam and Lebanon — have become "total" in conceptualization and execution.

For many Christians history has come full circle. Faced with the reality of total war, its strategies, and its weapons, the only appropriate response for those who would be followers of Christ becomes, once again, the absolute pacifism of the primitive Church. A world seemingly dedicated to its own annihilation offers no viable alternative to a rediscovered and renewed commitment to the nonviolence preached by its Founder. A worldly prudence which seeks security in the power and readiness to inflict total destruction upon any potential enemy regardless of the risk to creation's future must finally yield to the Scriptural assurance that His power is perfected in human infirmity and the promise that the gates of hell will not prevail.

Between the two world wars Roman Catholic pacifists (a contradiction in terms, some of their fellow communicants insisted) still put their case in the context of traditional post-Constantinian theology, rejecting war because it could no longer fit the conditions of the "just war." Often enough their arguments included an explicit disclaimer of absolute pacifism. Hiroshima shifted the balance. Some still use the "just war" formulation, but the widespread tendency is to dismiss the concept as a redundancy, a regrettable compromise of the purity of Christian witness that is only now being recognized and corrected.

Contemporary pacifists are usually not inclined to engage in elaborate theological disputation. They are content with the unambiguous conviction that war in its nature is (and probably has always been) irreconcilable with the spirit of Christianity, a position they believe confirmed in Scripture and given literal application in the witness of the early Christians. What their interpretation may lack in intellectual sophistication is more than balanced by a deepened spirituality and sense of emotional commitment. Total war, in short, has brought a rebirth of absolute pacifism.

"Lord, it is true. We are not on the right path." Pope Paul VI's lament in his 1970 World Day of Peace message finds its echo in the conviction held by Christians of the pacifist persuasion that the turning away from that "right path" came with the acceptance of the concept of justifiable war. The rediscovery of that path, they will insist, requires a new theology of peace and nonviolence along with the readiness to accept sacrifice and suffering, even persecution, as the price for renouncing war and its atrocities.

Such a return to the Church's beginnings with the possibility of a second "Age of Martyrs" raises the question as to whether modern Christians are prepared to meet such a challenge. The story of Franz Jaegerstaetter, a simple Austrian peasant, gives reason to hope we can. In 1943 this heroic man, married and the father of three small children, was beheaded in Berlin for his refusal to serve in the armed forces of a regime he considered evil. Everyone — family, friends, neighbors, priests, even his bishop — counseled him to "do his duty" as ordered, but nothing could shake his conviction that his first duty was to God and his Church regardless of the cost.

There is no way of knowing how many others may have died like Jaegerstaetter and for the same reasons only to perish without record.

Maximilian, too, was but one among many martyrs, most of whom are honored only in the anonymity of the Feast of All Saints. The point is that many more might have taken that stand had they been called to it by their spiritual leaders, and the course of history could have been changed. As it was, this simple man had to take his stand alone aided only by his faith, by his conscious identification with the saints and martyrs he had taken as models, and by his firm conviction that for being true to his conscience he would merit eternal reward in heaven.

There is one thing we do know, however. The peasant and any others who took that stand were more attuned to the true meaning of the Christian faith and promise than were the bishops who told the German faithful to fight for Folk and Fatherland as a Christian duty. Whatever else the war and its horrors may have accomplished, it exposed the utter irrelevance of the just war tradition to the reality of modern war. The extreme in futility was reached in the opinion of one learned theologian that any judgment as to whether the war was just or unjust had to await its end when "all the facts" would be in. In the meantime there was nothing to do but follow orders.

The Christian faced with the prospect of an even more horrible war, perhaps the ultimate war, cannot be satisfied with a theology which failed to recognize the injustice of Hitler's wars. They demand a better and truer answer, and for a growing number that answer is the complete renunciation of all war. In this they find encouragement in the words of John Paul II: "The horror of modern warfare — whether nuclear or not — makes it totally unacceptable as a means of settling differences between nations."

5.
Peace, War and the Christian Conscience

Catholic opponents of war, wherever they are, must come to terms with the tragic truth that the "universality" of our Church has usually found expression in too ready a willingness to endorse and support participation in wars and (for the past 1500 years at least) a reluctance to challenge its faithful to give active witness instead to its Founder's teachings of peace and nonviolence.

Something of a re-awakening began in the interval between the two World Wars. In great part due to the writings of the Dominican, Father Franziskus Stratmann O.P., there developed what might be described as a "Thomist" or "neo-Scholastic" pacifism. While not yet accepting the "absolutism" of the so-called "peace churches" with their total rejection of all violence and war, this new theological interpretation recognized the impossibility of fitting the weapons and strategies of modern warfare into the traditional concept of the "just war" and its conditions. In Germany Stratmann joined with the later martyred Max Josef Metzger to found The Peace League of German Catholics, which soon claimed over a thousand local units and many thousands of members and was deemed enough of a "problem" to merit the honor of being one of the first, if not the very first, denominationally identified organizations to be driven out of existence by the Gestapo once Hitler came to power. This modernized Thomism was the position of the British PAX Society as well.

In 1943 one of its officers, Stormont Murray, identified PAX as an organization which rejected "the idea of a justifiable war here and now" because "war today" failed to meet the "rigid conditions" which were required for the use of force to be "morally justifiable." The introduction of atomic warfare at Hiroshima and Nagasaki led E. I. Watkin, another PAX official, to declare that event finally eliminated all possibility of a "just war."

In the United States the Catholic Worker movement accepted and used such arguments in its monthly paper, but its position was much closer to the "peace church" absolutism. Its basic ideology stressed the striving for perfection "as our heavenly Father is perfect" and the commitment to sacrificial love and the spiritual and corporal works of mercy. Even in a "just war," its members would hold, the Christian was called to go beyond justice to love the enemy. As one of the intellectual leaders of the conscientious objectors assigned to the camp sponsored by the Worker put it, the "just war" principles in their Aristotelian/Stoic origins represented the ethic required of "the good pagan." Christians, he insisted, are called to a higher ethic.

Not that this represented the unanimous position of the camp population, it should be noted. Though campers who had been actively associated with Catholic Worker houses of hospitality dominated camp administration and promoted their "perfectionist" point of view, the wide range of backgrounds of the men involved was reflected in positions ranging from strict "just war" adherents (who held the war in progress failed to meet the required conditions) to advocates of absolute pacifism (admittedly sometimes more the product of emotion than theological argument) with a few who were conscientious objectors because they believed the U.S. was on the wrong side and should have been united with the fascist forces opposing atheistic Bolshevism. Arguments, as one might expect, were almost continuous and usually quite lively.

At best, a very strange band of "prophets" but this nascent "Catholic peace movement" opposing World War II in Britain and the United States may have quite *accidentally* laid the foundation without which the more theologically sophisticated and effective Catholic peace movement could not have gained the influence *and the respect* it enjoys in both countries today.

World War II ended in a storm of theological confusion. The two atomic bombings merely capped the demonic escalation of "conventional" terror and obliteration bombings, and the victors were united only in their suspicion of each other's motives and intentions. Some of the military and political leaders on the "democratic" side were even prepared, if necessary, to move on to Moscow to complete the job. A few, as we know, were ready to make common cause with the defeated enemy in doing so.

In his final years Pope Pius XII gave cause for hope in his apparent condemnation of the new "advances" (if one may use that term) in atomic, bacteriological and chemical warfare and, by inference if not by official declaration, narrowing the conditions for "justifiable" war to only one: defense against unjust aggression. Unfortunately, from the pacifist's perspective at least, he also all but excluded conscientious objection as a legitimate option for the Catholic. To complicate Rome's record still further, it is now quite clear that a rather dubious "underground railroad" operated in the immediate postwar years — whether the Pope was aware of it or not — to facilitate the escape of prominent Nazis and others suspected of war crimes. This, coupled with the controversy over Pius's failure or refusal to publicly condemn Hitler's infamous "Final Solution," left the Church suspect of indifference or, to some, complicity.

This was the time and the setting in which the Catholic peace movement was reborn. British PAX, the Catholic Worker, and the few other groups which had persevered through the bad days of the war now found a more receptive hearing and support in continuing what they had been trying to do all along. They were joined by new groups, some with more sharply focused or limited interests and goals. In the United States, some of the men who had been in alternate service joined with Dorothy Day and several of the Workers who wanted to concentrate more heavily on peace concerns and formed an American PAX Society modeled on its British counterpart. In Germany the remnants of the former *Friedensbund*, after futile efforts to resurrect the Stratmann movement, divided between the newly created Pax Christi and the more left-oriented Pax Vobis, with the former winning out in the competition for Catholic support.

Founded in 1945 by Bishop Theas of Lourdes at the instigation of a group of French laity, Pax Christi began as a movement for reconciliation between French and German veterans. It has since broadened in scope both in terms of international representation and, more important perhaps, in its definition of purpose.

Caution and reverence for protocol are still much in evidence at the organization's international meetings, but (and this is in great part due to the contributions of the English-speaking sections, I make bold to say) its early reluctance to tackle "touchy" subjects has largely disappeared. As a movement it may not yet merit the designation of "crusade" employed by Pius XII when he gave it his blessing and commendation; still it is engaged in the works he praised: "spreading everywhere the Christian concept of peace and creating, by the prayers of its members and circulation of its literature, an atmosphere of universal understanding which will be the basis for a true and lasting reconciliation between men and nations."

It stretches the point to suggest that the Pope's praise conferred "official" ecclesiastical status upon the movement. Even so, its international character makes Pax Christi the most significant Catholic peace movement of our time. Through it the spirit of British PAX and its American clone — both of which have become national sections of the international movement — remains active. There has been a highly significant change, however. The emphasis on the "just war" tradition, even as modified by Stratmann and his followers, is now overshadowed (though not eliminated) by the more thoroughgoing rejection of all violence and war that characterized the earliest centuries of Church history. A companion change is the extent to which the Christian witness against war has shifted from intellectual disputation to a concern for means of translating that witness into more effective action.

These changes, of course, have taken place in the broader context of that "new approach" to war called for by the Second Vatican

Council and anticipated in John XXIII's great peace encyclical, *Pacem in Terris*. Since that watershed document was first issued, there has been a steady stream of papal statements — some calling for the abolition of nuclear war and denouncing the arms race; others affirming the legitimacy of conscientious objection and encouraging the search for alternatives to war in the pursuit of international peace and justice. These statements in their turn have been echoed (sometimes improved upon) by similar appeals voiced by individual bishops and formalized in pastoral directives issued by national hierarchies. The 1983 pastoral letter of the U.S.hierarchy, *The Challenge of Peace: God's Promise and Our Response,* deserves particular acclaim in this respect. None of this was or could have been anticipated, even in wildest fantasy, by me and my fellow campers doing our civilian public service in World War II. Though the institutional Church may not yet have come as far or as fast as we may wish today, such statements provide an invaluable foundation and (if one may borrow a military term) "launching pad" upon which Pax Christi and others in the Catholic peace movement can base their future efforts.

We may take gratification (and pride too) in recognizing the fact of a two-way relationship in this: those statements and policies of the institutional Church might not be available as reinforcement for today's Catholic peace movement were it not for the earlier generation's stubborn perseverance in the days when it was unnoticed, unwanted, and ignored. It would be unwise, though, to make too much of that. The *real* cause of these welcome changes in the Church's attitudes and teachings regarding modern war are the changes in the nature of war itself, its weapons, and the inhuman strategies those weapons make possible. It is these, not simply the persuasive cogency of our arguments, which demonstrate once and for all the absurdity and irrelevance of the "just war" tradition today. Our task has been — and will continue to be — to make that point as insistently as possible so that, however much "prudence" and "pragmatic necessity" may seem to recommend silence in some future situation, the official leadership of a Church which claims to be the Mystical Body of Christ may never again be permitted to ignore or escape its responsibility to speak out.

The minor "victories" we can claim to this point should not give us too much comfort. Whatever satisfaction we take from the progress Pax Christi and the other segments of the peace movement have made since the end of World War II must be tempered by the awareness that the challenge still before us is greater now than it ever has been. The technology of modern warfare and the plans and preparations already under way to put it to use have developed a dynamic all their own. The depersonalization process which, psychologists tell us, must take place before one human being is made ready and willing to destroy another on command has been perfected and now extends that readiness to entire populations. Indeed, to the planet itself. The war in the Persian Gulf, blessedly brief though it was, gives ample demonstration of how human beings have become little more than expendable and replaceable appendages of technological killing machines.

It is right to take hope from the growing worldwide demand for significant steps toward disarmament and the ultimate elimination of war. The rediscovery by the major Christian religious communities of the mission to advance the cause of peace and nonviolence may be late and still incomplete; but this, too, is a source of hope. Nevertheless, that hope will disappear if we fail to translate these goals and values into the awareness and acceptance by ordinary men and women of their personal responsibility to do what they can individually to reverse the trend toward war while there is still time. But this, I fear, will not be possible unless present assumptions of helplessness are replaced by a renewed commitment to the potential and power of the individual conscience.

Shakespeare thought he had the word for it. "Conscience," he has Hamlet lament, "makes cowards of us all." All too often the behavior of Christians — and this has been especially true of *Catholic* Christians — gives evidence that they agree.

Consider, if you will, the parents who are ready to "disown" sons who choose to become conscientious objectors or, if they do not go quite that far, voice strong parental disapproval and concern about the shame such a decision could bring upon the family. Not that this is too widespread a problem, perhaps.

Few young Catholics who might be called up in some future draft are even aware that conscientious objection is an option whose legitimacy has been affirmed by all the recent popes, by the Vatican Council, by national hierarchies. They have not learned this in their local parishes or, for that matter, in their Catholic high schools and institutions of higher learning. Even if they had, they might not be impressed by that fact or by knowing that John Paul II has gone so far as to praise conscientious objection as "a sign of maturity."

According to the Fathers of Vatican II, conscience is "a law written by God" in human hearts, the "most secret core and sanctuary" where one is "alone with God." Part of the task of a Catholic peace movement is to make this meaningful and immediately relevant to every person who professes to claim the name of Christian. There is no denying that being true to one's conscience will seldom be easy, that it is often costly and even dangerous. This merely increases the vital importance of getting the message across. The U.S. bishops in their 1983 peace pastoral spelled it out in its fullest implications: "To be a Christian, according to the New Testament," they declared, "is not simply to believe with one's mind, but also to become a doer of the word, a wayfarer with and a witness to Jesus. This means, of course, that we never expect complete success within history and that we must regard as normal even the path of persecution and the possibility of martyrdom."

Franz Jaegerstaetter knew that. This "ordinary" peasant, beheaded in 1943 for refusing to serve in Hitler's army, went to his death certain that no one outside his village would ever know about him or his sacrifice. This did not bother him too much because, in his mind, it was simply a matter between him and his God. Nothing more. We know now he was wrong about the impact his sacrifice would have, but had he known, it would have made no difference to him. Although everyone who knew of his intention — family, friends, neighbors, priests and even his bishop — pleaded with him to consider the needs of his wife and family, to "do his duty" and not throw his life away in pointless sacrifice, he persisted.

Today he is honored as a national hero in his beloved Austria and as a prospective saint by his even more deeply beloved Church for his refusal to violate his conscience.

Shakespeare was wrong. Dead wrong!

It is the role of conscience to make *heroes* of us all by helping us to become the Christians we can be and are called to be. Cowards are those who surrender moral judgment to experts and those in power, who "go along" when dissent or refusal seems pointless and foolhardy. Christians living in what the bishops call "this new moment" would do well to take Jaegerstaetter as the example of the sacrifice conscience may demand of us all if the war that is forbidden becomes a reality.

The demands of conscience are not limited to the young people who may be called upon to reject military service in a war they consider immoral or unjust. Modern society is so tightly integrated that no member can escape being involved in whatever is done in the name of the whole. In societies like ours which at least profess a commitment to democratic ideals and representational procedures this involvement imposes a measure of personal responsibility for the policies and actions of those we choose to conduct our affairs. No matter how much we may prefer to ignore the fact and its implications, how each of us exercises this responsibility should find its guidelines in that law written in our hearts.

This applies, of course, to every relationship we have with one another, but it is easier to state the principle linking private conscience with social responsibility than to apply it in particular circumstances. There are always competing values and obligations to be considered. It then becomes the role of conscience to help us determine the order of priority among them. For the Christian faced with the need to define and resolve his or her responsibilities relating to war and peace, the problem becomes most acute. It is not too much to say that, given what is now at stake — the very real prospect of that "global suicide" Thomas Merton warned against — it could determine our chances for eternal salvation.

Merton's answer in the face of that danger, written a quarter-century ago, is still as valid as it was then: "It is no longer possible or right to leave all decisions to a largely anonymous power elite that is driving us all, in our passivity, toward ruin. We have to make ourselves heard." The important thing is that as citizens and as Christians we bear an inescapable obligation to do something. And once our decision is made, there is the further and continuing obligation to periodically re-assess whether we are doing all we can.

It is not only the opponents of current policies or conscientious objectors who face that continuing obligation. Those who support those policies and endorse the current state of preparations for war have even more difficult choices to make. Since their responsibility is more direct, it is more crucial that they be sensitive to restraints or any doubts they may entertain in that "secret core and sanctuary" of their souls.

This is especially true, of course, for individuals who accept or volunteer for service in the armed forces. Their moral responsibility does not end when they put on the uniform; if anything that is only the beginning. Participation in war and preparation for war must always be *conscientious* participation, never unquestioning obedience to those in command. At times this may impose a definite *obligation* to disobey. If, as the bishops' pastoral put it, "No Christian can rightfully carry out orders or policies deliberately aimed at killing noncombatants," logic should imply that the Christian serviceperson ought to avoid or reject military assignments where orders or policies that are certain to bring such results are most likely to be encountered. On nuclear-armed submarines. In long-range bomber forces. In chemical or bacteriological warfare units. And there should no longer be the slightest doubt that anyone presented with orders to turn the key or press the button to "take out" a number of population centers would be faced with a severe crisis of conscience.

In the Second World War a German general, morally disturbed by Hitler's decision to invade Norway, gave advance notice of the plans to the Allied forces. In the military scale of values, this was high treason. To General Oster, though, it was an obligation in conscience. Would an American or British officer of equal rank privy to secret plans to launch a "decapitating" first strike against Moscow or some other "enemy" capital be prepared to do the same? Would the Catholic chaplain of the unit assigned to that task be prepared to counsel the men in his spiritual charge to refuse?

This is no idle question. *The day may come when the last remaining hope for the survival of the human race, the last safeguard against Merton's "moral evil second only to the Crucifixion," may be the conscience of some disobedient soldier.* That is why we must insist that our Church, along with all the other religious communions, provide the kind of spiritual guidance and assistance that is needed *now* to form and strengthen the consciences of those who might be called upon to make that fateful decision.

Everyone who would be a peacemaker or even just a seeker after peace must assume part of the burden of reminding others, by word or example, of the responsibility we all share for the future existence of the world and all its inhabitants.

We must be prepared to prod the religious leadership to action when it seems too willing to leave essential moral decisions to military or political authority.

Fifty years have passed since a handful of disorganized and contentious conscientious objectors represented what passed for the "active Catholic peace movement" in the United States. We were not prophets, perhaps, but we were pioneers. *The Catholic C.O.*, a newspaper published on a very erratic schedule, carried a legend on its masthead that nicely sums up the challenge that still faces today's Catholic peace movement: *We hope that war will be overcome through the Church, and even if, after two thousand years, this hope is still unfulfilled, we still hope and go on knocking at the door like the importunate man in the Gospel.*

That hope persists. We are still knocking and must and will go on knocking until that door, now slightly ajar, is finally opened all the way.

6.
Catholic Responses to the Holocaust

Any serious discussion of the Holocaust must begin with the frank admission that the Christian communities, within Germany and outside, failed to meet or even recognize their moral obligation to give effective witness against one of history's greatest crimes. As a Catholic, I cannot ignore the fact that my Church shared in that failure by its sins of omission and even, in far too many instances, through direct sins of commission on the part of its members. This is, moreover, a failure that defies accurate or even adequate measurement. No research into the subject, especially at this point almost half a century later, can be based on more than an accidental sampling, remembered impressions, piecemeal accounts of isolated fragments of the tragic story.

By and large, I am convinced, the Catholic world has come to terms with the fact of failure, though not without a certain amount of defensive pleading and even some attempts at self-justification. There is reason for this, of course. For one thing it is the Roman Catholic Church that has been the target for the earliest and sharpest criticism. Altogether too much has been made, for instance, of the Catholic origins of Hitler and many of his chief henchmen, ignoring the perfectly obvious evidence that most of them had abandoned any pretension to whatever confessional commitments they may once have had. The 1933 Concordat and the aura of legitimacy it provided the Nazi state provides a much stronger basis for criticism, but even here the fault has been exaggerated and too little allowance has been made for the fact that its future ramifications and consequences could not be foreseen at the time. The criticism and attacks reached a peak of intensity in the worldwide "Hochhuth controversy" in the course of which a valid historical question was distorted into an overly simplified and essentially unjust effort to implicate Pope Pius XII as having a share of direct personal responsibility for the "Final Solution." Finally, there are the more recent allegations — and these, too, are apparently valid to some extent — that Catholic relief agencies facilitated the escape of some of the Nazi criminals. In the eyes of some this has become further evidence of institutional Catholic complicity and collaboration with the Third Reich and its evils. Within Germany itself, such charges were perhaps too easily exploited by the so-called *Linkskatholiken* ("Catholics of the Left") in their political opposition to the Christian Democratic Union and what they regarded as a threatened union of Church and State in the postwar Adenauer era.

The passage of time ought to enable us to put these issues in better perspective. It is encouraging that more recognition is being given by historians of the Nazi period to the other side of the grim story, the often inspiring record of assistance that was given and the Jewish lives that were saved through Christian intervention. This record is incomplete and, sad to say, must always remain so; but at least there is less danger today of its being overlooked or forgotten altogether. There is no reason to doubt that the final balance, when it is finally struck, will still be weighted heavily with the disgrace of Christian failure. Granting that, it will still be possible to claim that those who broke the pattern at the cost of grave personal risk and sacrifice may have redeemed the day. After all, in the biblical account, ten just men would have been enough to save the Cities of the Plain. There were many more than ten in Nazi Germany.

We are most concerned here, and rightly so, with the reasons why there were not more. In the final analysis, those reasons must lie in the motivations and perceptions of each individual involved and these, as noted earlier, are beyond recapture. Even so, it is permissible and appropriate for the sociologist to try to at least set the issue in its broader social dimensions. Foremost among these, of course, is the extent to which Catholic attitudes and behavior toward the Jews of Germany and, later, the Jews of the other nations unfortunate enough to come under Nazi domination were infected and shaped by anti-Semitism. That this played an important part in the Catholic record of failure is clear. Nor was its influence limited to Catholics of lesser rank. It may have received its crudest expression there, but there is little doubt that it also reached in subtler and more insidious ways into the higher levels of society and the Church as well.

It is important, however, to distinguish between different forms of this ideological disease. Most obvious, if only because it is most familiar, is what we may describe as "theological" anti-Semitism, the product of what Jules Isaac and others have traced to "the teaching of contempt." This, it is safe to assume, would have had its most telling impact upon the fundamentalist-oriented peasantry (the kind of thing one still encounters, for example, in the Oberammergau Passion Play) and, at the other end of the scale, among ecclesiastical professionals.

It would be a serious mistake to stop with this. Allowances must be made as well for a "cultural" anti-Semitism, one derived from social practices and values that had lost all specifically religious content and which permeated the more sophisticated circles of German society. Finally there was the "anti-Semitism of the resentful," the disadvantaged — and in particular the urban disadvantaged who attributed their economic distress to the prosperity of others and who were especially susceptible to exaggerated assumptions concerning the prosperity of the Jews. All three strains were intermingled, each reinforcing the other two to some extent. Still it is useful to recognize the crucial differences among them in making any assessment of the part played by anti-Semitism in the failure of Christians, particularly Catholic Christians, to meet the moral challenge presented by the Final Solution.

But anti-Semitism is not a sufficient, or even necessary, cause of that failure, as too many are inclined to believe. We are dealing with a social phenomenon of far greater complexity than so simple an explanation would suggest. Even when we limit consideration to those sins of commission — that is, active participation in the extermination program — other explanatory factors must be taken into account. Whether one considers Franz Stangl, the (non-practicing) Catholic commandant of Treblinka or the (possibly still practicing) Catholic on guard detail, those other factors may have carried far greater weight than any animosity, conscious or unconscious, toward their victims as Jews.

With Stangl, as we learn in Gitta Sereny's *Into That Darkness,* a consuming ambition for career recognition and advancement, combined with a traditionally narrow definition of "duty," enabled him to put his actions in the context of "professionalism" while remaining indifferent to the ideological (much less *moral*) implications of the process in which he played so significant a part. This same kind of reasoning would have carried over to the guard as well, but in his case the added desire to avoid more hazardous service could have been far more compelling a motivation than any personal dedication to his *Fuehrer's* crazy vision of a "judenfrei" Europe.

To propose these alternative explanations (and there are others which might be offered) is not to imply that they justify or in any way lessen personal culpability for the crimes in which both Stangl and his hypothetical subordinate were willing collaborators. Indeed, one might go so far as to feel more compassion (dare one call it that?) for the misguided villain who did commit those crimes out of a fanatic commitment to some distorted scheme of values than for those others who merely accepted orders and performed their "duties" totally indifferent to the murderous rationale behind those orders.

The really crucial problem, however, concerns the sins of *omission.* The actual perpetrators of the Holocaust could be tracked down and punished — though, of course, relatively few actually were. No such action or reprisal need be anticipated by the great majority of German citizens who stood by in silence. Here again, it would be unfair to assign a greater burden of guilt or responsibility to

Catholics. Their sins of omission were matched by Protestant Christians as well as by Germans of no religious persuasion at all. What is different in their case, however, is the presumed availability of institutional mechanisms which could have operated and *should* have operated to produce another outcome. This is where Hochhuth's dramatic (*The Deputy*) indictment of Pius for his alleged refusal to publicly condemn the Final Solution finds its limited measure of validity. Why, we must ask, did these mechanisms not work? A major part of the blame, obviously enough, lies with the Pope and bishops for failing to bring them into play, but this does not diminish the responsibility of the individual Catholic to form and follow his, or her, own conscience. And why did the faithful fall so short of this ideal? The first answer is the one most frequently advanced: ignorance of what was going on. However much we may discount the extent to which this ignorance did prevail, we cannot dismiss it altogether. That Eichmann and his cohorts went to great lengths to shroud their activities in secrecy is a matter of historical record, and there is good reason to believe the effort was successful to some extent. Beyond this, there was the ignorance traceable to the ordinary German citizen's prudent *desire not to know* which led him to close his eyes to what was taking place and, where this was not possible, to dismiss the evidence of his own eyes out of simple disbelief or refusal to believe. Culpable ignorance this may have been, but ignorance nonetheless.

Those who did know could easily find other reasons for remaining silent and uninvolved. This would be easiest for those who were susceptible to anti-Semitism: for them, it would have been a matter of "just deserts" and they would have little inclination to interfere or disapprove. The same disposition would govern the responses of those Germans, anti-Semites or not, who were caught up in the national adulation of Hitler as charismatic leader. Still others could simply take refuge in the traditional theological teachings which counseled obedience to lawful authority and regard it as beyond their obligation or competence to question the policies or programs of the nation's leaders.

The most troubled, and troubling, category would be those Catholics who knew *and* disapproved. In their case other obvious considerations would apply. If nothing else, the threat to their own and their families' safety and well-being would operate to discourage most of them from giving open expression to their disapproval or taking any steps to oppose those policies or programs. Thus one professor, a Catholic, confessed to me the shame and guilt he had felt after encountering and ignoring a Jewish former colleague who had been reduced to cleaning the streets of their university town. The professor may not have been a hero, but we should be able to understand the lack of heroism and, perhaps, even allow some credit, however slight, for the sense of guilt that remained with him more than a decade after the end of World War II.

This brings us back to that Hochhuth problem. Given the dominant role assigned to ecclesiastical authority in the structure of the Roman Catholic Church, it is not unreasonable to argue that the German bishops and the Pope should have recognized a moral responsibility to marshal the faithful into effective opposition to the Final Solution. But this merely elevates the foregoing exploration of the reasons for failure to a new level. One crucial difference, however, is immediately relevant: ignorance was surely not a factor here, though whether these church leaders were aware of the full dimensions of the ongoing atrocity is open to question. Similarly, with the possible exception of a very few bishops (and in almost every case this held true for only a time), support for Hitler and the Nazi movement can be excluded as a viable explanation. We may assume that fears for personal safety and well-being operated to counsel restraint; however, when other issues on which bishops and pope were courageously outspoken are taken into account, it would appear that any such fears were not a major consideration.

On the other hand, it is tragically clear from official statements and acts that leading members of the German hierarchy were influenced by patriotic enthusiasm and nationalistic sentiments. An even more grievous admission to make, it is clear that they shared to a regrettable extent those culturally imposed and theologically reinforced definitions of the Jew as "alien" to the Germanic tradition and "deniers" of Christ. That they did not and would not have approved the Nazi excesses can be taken for granted. Unfortunately, their disapproval was evidently not accorded an especially high priority among their many objections to Hitler and his regime.

Their most pressing concern was the avoidance of reprisals which, they knew, would not be directed against their own persons but, rather, against the Church and the faithful entrusted to their care. This was certainly a legitimate worry, one firmly grounded in the bishops' awareness of the animosity directed against Catholicism by the Nazi leaders and sufficiently demonstrated by the experience of reprisal actions already suffered for relatively slight cause. The Concordat notwithstanding, these spiritual leaders had to recognize the possibility, indeed the probability, that any show of opposition would expose Germany's Catholics to punitive treatment as "enemies of the state." From our perspective, safely removed in time and space from the threats they faced, we may take issue with the bishops' surrender to prudence (if that is what it was) and argue the case for heroic protest and acceptance of the penalties as a more prophetic Christian witness. To the bishop struggling to keep his churches open and functioning in an aggressively anti-religious totalitarian society, the situation and the solution might not have been quite so clear.

Finally there is that most troubling balance to be struck in any attempt to analyze and understand the lack of effective Catholic response to the Holocaust. I refer, of course, to the role played (or not played) by papal authority. Those who have risen to the defense of Pius XII in response to the Hochhuth charges have stressed the pragmatic considerations which, they insist, explain and justify the Pope's apparent decision not to issue an explicit and formal condemnation. For one thing, they argue, it would have destroyed the carefully nurtured posture of ostensible neutrality and removed all prospect, slight though it may have been, of mediation or other papal intervention to end the war. This, beyond question, was the objective that held first priority as far as Pius was concerned.

Then, too, a formal condemnation of the Third Reich or its policies would only have served to expose Jews in Vatican safekeeping to certain and immediate arrest and deportation. This argument cannot be dismissed out of hand, and it takes on added force when one considers that such a public denunciation would almost certainly have had little or no actual effect in Germany and the occupied areas. True, it *might* have reduced the ignorance (assuming news of the condemnation was permitted to reach the German faithful). It *might* have helped to weaken or counteract those sentiments of loyalty to the nation or to the idealized *Fuehrer*. It might even have reduced or neutralized the continuing influence of religious and cultural anti-Semitism. Yet had all these objectives been served, the harsh fact remains that it is most unlikely that any papal call, no matter how strong in tone and specific in terms, would have succeeded in rallying the general Catholic population to prospective martyrdom. The majority of Germany's Catholics would not have dared nor wished to turn against their nation's leaders in the midst of an increasingly destructive war. Like it or not, the bishops (and Pope) must have realized that such a call to virtual martyrdom would almost certainly have gone unanswered.

Against such odds the *certainty* of more Jewish lives being lost as a result of the futile attempt cannot be lightly shunted aside. In strictly quantitative terms, it may be that the sacrifice of another two or three hundred Jews harbored in the Vatican would not seem too high a price to pay for righteous denunciation at a time when six million or more were being liquidated in the murder camps. In actuality, we now learn that many more Jewish lives were at stake. Until this point, our review has accentuated the negative, concentrating on the extent to which Catholics may have participated actively in the slaughter or were guilty of passive complicity through their silence. It is time to shift now to a more positive emphasis and acknowledge those who did refuse to go along and, in the process, succeeded in saving not just a few hundred but thousands of Jews from the Nazi horror.

The actual count of lives saved or a true measure of the risks involved for those who helped save them can never be known because these actions were of necessity conducted in secrecy. The unhappy Dutch experience, where public protest by religious leaders was met by an immediate escalation of the persecution, was enough to demonstrate the virtue of anonymity if demonstration were needed. This absence of written records, however, means that the story, if it is to be pieced together at all, depends on retrieving the facts through the techniques of oral history. Today, as memories fade and potential sources are lost through the attrition of death, much, probably most, of the history of that "saving remnant" has been lost.

In retrospect, it is clear that a more systematic attempt to uncover those facts should have been made after the war's end, but priority was given (and it is easy to understand why) to tracking down the guilty and their collaborators. We must be grateful for the stories we know, even as we bemoan the loss of those we will never know. It is well that we honor the memory of a Bernhard Lichtenberg, Cathedral provost in Berlin, who offended by adding prayers for the Jews to his evening services and died en route to Dachau; but in doing so, we ought to voice a prayer of thanksgiving as well for any other parish priests who, unknown to us and to history, may have added their public prayers for the welfare of persecuted Jews to his. There are moving accounts of how individual survivors were sheltered or "adopted" by sympathetic Christians, but little attention has been given to the background of institutional encouragement and support which may have made such seemingly isolated actions possible. A former activist in the "Zegota" underground in Poland confirmed that convents, schools, and other Catholic agencies played a crucial role — and always at the certain risk of being shut down were the occupation authorities to discover they were harboring Jewish youngsters and passing them off as Christian.

That such saving actions were conducted without some knowledge on the part of the surrounding Catholic community and support, possibly even direction, from ecclesiastical authorities is most unlikely. In the course of my own earlier research, I had the occasion to interview a number of Catholics in Freiburg-im-Breisgau who had operated a kind of "underground railroad," spiriting Jews across the Swiss border. They made it clear that their efforts were known to, and in part financially subsidized, by Cardinal Faulhaber of Munich. The only condition imposed was that such funds were always provided in cash and steps had to be taken to assure what, since Watergate, has become known as "deniability."

Alexander Ramati in his book, *The Assisi Underground: The Priests Who Rescued Jews,* describes in detail the extraordinary accomplishments of a Franciscan priest who was charged by his local bishop with the task of assisting Jewish refugees passing through Assisi to freedom. Before long he had established a center for counterfeiting identity papers and other official documents — an accomplishment, incidentally, that also involved the theft of the required seal from the local government office. In due course the Germans succeeded in choking off the escape route, and it became the priest's job to locate housing for an increasing number of "guests" in religious shelters. At his urging even the rigidly cloistered Poor Clares violated their Order's strict rule and permitted not only men but entire Jewish families to enter and live in their otherwise forbidden precincts.

It is an incredible story and one which might never have been known beyond the few sentences referring to Franciscan efforts in Pinchas Lapide's *Three Popes and the Jews*. Ramati learned about the operation as one of the first American war correspondents to enter Assisi when the Germans left; still it was not until 1972, *28 years later,* that he finally got around to fulfilling his intention to return and bring the story to public attention. As it was, it was too much of a "near thing." Before the book was published, Padre Rufino Niccacci, in whose words the recollected story is told, had died.

Niccacci, it is well to note, had already received a measure of recognition by being honored as a "Righteous Gentile" by Israel. Even so, this personal honor, well deserved though it most certainly was, is incomplete to the extent that it does not take full account of the official institutional involvement of the Catholic Church. It was a bishop who assigned Niccacci to the mission of helping and saving Jews. Is it not possible that the bishop in his turn was receiving some encouragement, even direction, from the Holy See — again in some unrecorded fashion to assure "deniability"?

Of course, to bring attention to the fact that there was a more heroic side to the Catholic response to the Holocaust and that some of that response benefited from and depended upon institutional support, does not contradict the overall assessment of the Catholic record as a moral failure. At best it merely confirms what we should have known all along: heroes were fewer than one might have hoped; that there were any at all is more than we have a right to demand. Throughout all the crises of human history, it has ever been thus.

This has some very important implications. That the world will continue to commemorate the Holocaust as a historical event of immeasurably tragic proportions should be a foregone conclusion. However, it is not enough to leave it at that. Beyond mere commemoration is the challenge to place the event in a broader context, to raise the more troubling questions and seek more profound answers concerning the human potential for good and evil. Too many have used the failure of the Christian churches as an easy justification for rejecting religion altogether, quite ignoring the fact that most of those who merited honor by their heroic opposition to the perpetrators of the Holocaust did so out of deep, personal religious commitment. Too often, too, Christians see the event and its commemoration as a vehicle for "celebrating" Christian guilt, as though others (including Jews in Germany and throughout the world) did not succumb to much the same complex of external pressures and internal weakness that conspired to produce the moral failure acknowledged here.

It in no way diminishes the horror, the immorality, even the uniqueness of the Holocaust to remind ourselves that it was not the first, nor even the latest, example of the wholesale instrumental destruction of human life to serve some immediate social purpose. The categories marked for such "socially therapeutic" extermination may differ. Sometimes they are national; other times racial or religious; increasingly, class. Nevertheless the underlying rationale remains essentially the same whether the particular victims be Jews, Armenians, Kulaks, Cambodians, or, to bring the issue closer to home, the six million lives (a truly ironic number!) terminated in our own country in the first six years following the Supreme Court's decision on abortion.

There are many, I know, who feel otherwise and reject any effort to generalize or universalize the Holocaust as tantamount to a betrayal of its victims. And to extend the application to divisively controversial issues like abortion and euthanasia may seem particularly offensive to some. The objections would be valid if one were simply to equate such private acts based on individual decisions with an officially planned and engineered program of mass genocide. That is not intended here.

However, in a sociological perspective, actions find their importance not only in themselves but, beyond this, as expressions of values and meanings. What the Holocaust reveals, then, is more than the fatal product of a few deranged minds in positions of unlimited power. Rather it testifies to a capacity to reduce the intrinsic value of human life itself to a purely utilitarian scale, to an expendable. Viewed in this context, the Holocaust is not only an event of near cosmic tragedy that is over and done with. It is an expression of a present threat of other and possibly greater holocausts that may lie ahead.

If there is any lesson to be drawn from the grim record, it is that when such actions occur in the future — as they probably will —

they must never again be met with silence or equivocation on the part of those who would call themselves religious, specifically Christian, more specifically Catholic. That we are likely to fail again as we have failed in the past is true enough, but we will have succeeded to the extent that we can increase the number of those who will recognize an obligation to give witness, to voice the conscience of humankind regardless of the costs or risks involved.

Thirty years ago Christian Geisler, a young German writer, drew a chilling parallel between Auschwitz and Hiroshima. As he put it, both were empirical demonstrations of the horrendous capacity for justifying the mass destruction of living human beings. Any mind even capable of formulating such justifications, he insisted, was corrupt. And he went on to add the sad judgment: "This corruption is general."

The final and surest test of whether we have or have not come to terms with the Holocaust becomes frighteningly simple. It is the extent to which each of us is able to free himself, or herself, from that general corruption of mind and, even more, what each of us is doing to counteract it.

7.
A Religious Pacifist Looks at Abortion

Prudence, if nothing else, would seem to dictate that a celibate male, especially one committed to pacifism, should avoid getting embroiled in controversy with the women's liberation crowd. Ordinarily I would be all set to go along with this and not only for reasons of such prudential restraint. I am in general agreement with the movement's objectives and principles and more than ready to give it the benefit of almost every doubt — even though I do wish at times that its principal spokesmen (?) could be a little more, if not "ladylike," at least gentlemanly in their rhetoric and tone. But these are minor reservations.

There is one point of substance, however, on which I must register strong disagreement, and that is the increasing emphasis being placed on "free abortion on demand" as a principal plank in the liberationist's platform. From my perspective as a religious pacifist, I find this proposal thoroughly abhorrent; and I am disturbed by the willingness of so many who share my political and theological approach in most respects to go along with or condone a practice which so clearly contradicts the values upon which that approach is based.

In the past I have criticized "establishment" Christians, in particular official Catholic ecclesiastical and theological spokesmen, for their hypersensitivity to the evil of killing the unborn and their almost total disregard of the evil of "post-natal" abortion in the form of the wholesale destruction of human life in war. The argument works both ways and with equal force: those of us who oppose war cannot be any less concerned about the destruction of human life in the womb.

In discussing this issue from a pacifist standpoint I do not intend to enter upon two controversies which, though clearly related to the problem of abortion, are somewhat peripheral to my essential concern for life and the reverence for life. Thus, the whole question of the morality of contraception, obviously one of the alternatives to abortion as a means of population control, involves moral principles of an altogether different order. More closely related but also excluded from consideration is the legal question, that is whether or not anti-abortion legislation now on the statute books should be repealed, modified, or retained. One can argue, as I shall here, that abortion is immoral and still recognize compelling practical and theoretical reasons for not using state authority to impose a moral judgment that falls so far short of universal acceptance within the political community. On the other hand, there are equally compelling arguments upholding legal prohibition of what has long been considered by many to be a form of murder; and this takes on added force to the extent that repeal of laws already in effect will be interpreted as official authorization of the hitherto forbidden practice. Since the intention here is to discuss the objections to abortion itself, this very important legal question will be left for others to debate and resolve.

Nor will I comment upon what I consider the tactical blunder on the part of the liberationists to "borrow trouble" by making so touchy an issue — on emotional as well as moral grounds — a central part of their program. I must, however, reject the rationale that is usually advanced to support their demands, the "property rights" line which holds that because a woman's body is "her own," she and she alone must be left free to decide what is to be done about the developing fetus. Leaving aside the obvious fact that the presence of the fetus suggests a decision that could have been made earlier, this line of argument represents a crude reversion to the model of *laissez-faire* economics Catholics of a liberal or radical persuasion have long since repudiated. Even if one were to accept the characterization of a woman's body as "property" (is it not one of the liberationists' complaints that men and man-made laws have reduced her to that status?), the claim to absolute rights of use and disposal of that property could not be taken seriously. The owner of a badly needed residential building is not, or at least *should not be* free to evict his tenants to suit a selfish whim or to convert his property to some frivolous or non-essential use. In such a case we would insist upon the traditional distinction which describes property as private in ownership but social in use.

To use another example, the moral evil associated with prostitution does not lie solely, perhaps not even primarily, in the illicit sex relationship but, rather, in the degradation of a person to precisely this status of a "property" available for "use" on a rental or purchase basis. It is a tragic irony that the advocates of true and full personhood for women have chosen to provide ideological justifications for attitudes which have interfered with recognition of that personhood in the past.

This is not to say, of course, that a woman does not have prior rights over her own body but only that the exercise of those rights must take into account the rights of others. In monogamous marriage this would preclude a wife's "freedom" to commit adultery (a principle, it should be unnecessary to add, which applies to the husband as well). Similarly, in the case of a pregnancy in wedlock, the husband's rights concerning the unborn child must be respected too; indeed, even in a pregnancy out of wedlock, the putative father retains parental rights to the extent that he is ready to assume his share of responsibility for the child's future needs. In both cases, and this is the crux of the argument, of course, the rights of the unborn child, perhaps the most important claimant of all, must be respected and protected.

These categories of rights, I insist, are not to be put in any "property rights" or similar economic frame of reference. They represent elementary human rights arising out of an intimacy of union between responsible persons which transcends purely utilitarian or proprietary considerations. The governing consideration as far as the unborn child is concerned is simply this: when do these rights come into existence? The answer offered here, and I think it is the only answer compatible with a pacifist commitment, is that they exist at the moment of conception marking the beginning of the individual's life processes.

This has nothing to do with the old theological arguments over whether or not the soul can be said to be present at conception; it rests completely upon the determination of whether or not there is now something "living" in the sense that, given no induced or spontaneous interferences, it will develop into a human person. We know for certain that this fertilized ovum is not going to develop into a dog or cat or anything else; whatever its present or intervening states, it will at the end emerge as a human child. One need only consider the usual response to a spontaneous or accidental termination of a *wanted* pregnancy. The sorrow of the prospective parents, a sorrow shared by friends and relatives alike, testifies not only to the fact that something has "died" but also that this "something" was human.

So, too, with the medical arguments over when the fetus becomes "viable" and, therefore, eligible for birth. It is the life that is present, not the organism, which should concern us most. Once we agree that society's origin and purpose lie in the fulfillment of human capacities and needs, we have established the basis for a reverence for life which goes far beyond such purely technical determination. Should a life once begun be terminated (whether before or after the point of viability) because the prospective mother did not have adequate food or care or because she was forced by the demands of her social or economic condition to undergo excessive physical or psychological strain, we would have no problem about charging society with a failure to meet its responsibility. There is no reason to change this judgment when the termination is brought about by deliberate act, either to avoid some personal inconvenience or to serve what may be rationalized into the "greater good" of the family unit or, as the eugenicist might put it, society as a whole. Just as rights begin with the beginning of the life process, so does society's obligation to protect them.

Recently a new and somewhat terrifying "viability" test has been proposed in arguments supporting abortion. No longer is it to be the stage of physiological development which determines whether or not life is to be terminated but rather the degree to which "personhood" has emerged or developed. Although strict logic might suggest that personhood can be established only after the fetus has entered upon its extra-uterine existence (that is, after the child has been born) advocates are apparently willing to extend it back into the later weeks of pre-natal development as well.

Two objections to this test should be immediately obvious. In the first place (and the "generous allowance" of pre-natal personhood serves as a good illustration of this point), we are caught up with the same old problems of judgments that plagued the older viability standards: if the fetus is to be considered viable at x-weeks, what about the day before that period is completed? If personhood can be manifested in the pre-natal period when, let us say, fetuses can be compared in terms of differential activity, what about the hour before such differences can be noticed. Is more activity a sign that personhood is advanced, or might the absence of much activity be a sign of equal, though different, emergence of personhood?

The second objection is even more troubling. Under the old notion of physiological viability, the child once born was unquestionably viable. The same may not be true — or may not remain so in the face of changing social definitions — once the emergence or development of personhood is the measure. My experience as a conscientious objector in World War II doing alternate service at an institution for the mentally retarded introduced me to literally hundreds of individuals whose state of retardation was such that they were often described as "animals" or even "vegetables" by members of the institutional staff. Later, working in a hospital for mental diseases, I attended paretic and senile patients who had reached the state of regression and psychological deterioration at which the same terms could be applied to them and their behavior. However ardent and sincere the disclaimers may be, applying the test of personhood to the unborn is certain to open the way to pressures to apply that same test to the already born. In this sense, then, abortion and euthanasia are ideological twins.

In the old theological formulations of the problem, the condemnation of abortion was justified in terms of the "sanctity" or "intrinsic worth" of human life. Today much of the argument supporting abortion rests upon similar abstractions applied now to the intrinsic worth of the prospective mother's life or of siblings whose living standards and life chances might be threatened by the additional pregnancy. These are valid concerns and deserve serious and sympathetic understanding; and society does have a responsibility to find answers to these problems that do not involve the sacrifice of the human life that has begun. Pacifism and opposition to abortion converge here, for both find their ultimate justification in the Christian obligation to revere human life and its potential and to respect all of the rights associated with it.

The developmental model used by those who propose emergence of personhood as the test is basically sound, but as used by the advocates of abortion it becomes a logical enormity arguing for a development from an undefined or unstipulated beginning. A more consistent approach would see human life as a continuity from the point of clinically determined conception to the point of clinically determined death. This physiological life-span is then convertible to an existential framework as a developmental pattern of dependence relationships: at the earliest stages of a pregnancy the dependence is total; as the fetus develops, it takes on some of its own functions; at birth, its bodily functions are physiologically independent, but existential dependency is still the child's dominant condition. The rest of the pattern is obvious enough. As the individual matures and achieves the fullness of personhood, both functional and behavioral independence become dominant (though never total; culture and its demands must be taken into account). Finally, advanced age and physical decline returns him to a state of dependency which may, at the end, approximate that of earliest childhood.

Society's responsibilities to the individual stand in inverse relationship to the growth and decline of individual independence and autonomy. It would follow, then, that the immorality of abortion (and euthanasia as well) lies precisely in the fact that they propose to terminate the life process when the dependency is most total, that it would do so with the approval or authorization (possibly at the direction?) of society, that it would seek to justify this betrayal of society's responsibility on purely pragmatic grounds. The various claims made for the social utility of abortion (reducing the threat of overpopulation and now pollution; sparing the already disadvantaged family the strain of providing for yet another mouth to feed; etc.) or the even less impressive justifications in terms of personal and all too often selfish benefits to the prospective parent(s) have to be put in this context; and once they are they lose most of their force.

The earlier reference to the sorrow caused by the loss through miscarriage of a wanted child does not obscure the fact that most abortion proposals are concerned with preventing the birth of unwanted children. No one will deny that being regarded as an unwanted intruder in the family circle will be psychologically if not always physically harmful, but there should be other solutions to this problem than "sparing" the intruder this unpleasantness by denying him or her life in the first place. If a child is "unwanted" before conception, science has provided sufficient means for avoiding the beginning of the life process.

Since the sexual enlightenment burst upon us a generation or so ago, we have replaced the old Victorian notions about the "mystery of sex" with a kind of mechanistic assumption that the human being is the helpless victim of chemistry and unconscious impulses, an assumption which reduces sexual intercourse to a direct, natural, and almost compulsive response to stimuli and situations. The other side of this particular coin is the not so hidden danger that the human being will be redefined in strictly biological terms, a largely accidental event brought into being by the union of two adult organisms acting in response to that irresistible urge. This is reflected in many of the statements made by advocates of abortion in their references to the conceived child as a "fertilized ovum." The term is perfectly accurate in the strictly physiological sense; in the Christian perspective, however, it leaves something to be desired.

The act of intercourse, like any other human act, is and must remain subject to human responsibility. This means that those who enter upon it should consider the possible consequences of the act and acknowledge responsibility for those consequences if and when they come to pass. Ideally this would mean that unwanted children would not be conceived; where the ideal is not achieved — or where the participants change their minds after the child is conceived — it will be society's obligations to assume the responsibility for the new life that has been brought into being.

Unwanted pregnancies resulting from a freely willed and voluntary act of sexual intercourse are one thing; those resulting from rape require special consideration. Even here, I would hold, the reverence for life which forms the basis of this pacifist rejection of abortion would preclude the intentional termination of the life process begun under such tragic circumstances. The apparent harshness of this position may be mitigated somewhat by reflecting that pregnancies attributable to true rape (or incest) represent a small proportion of the unwanted. Certainly they do not constitute a large enough proportion to justify the emphasis placed upon them by proponents of abortion. This provides small consolation to the victim who has already undergone the traumatic experience of the assault itself and must still suffer the consequences of an act for which she bears no active responsibility. Nevertheless, the life that has begun is a human life and must be accorded the same rights and protection associated with the life resulting from normal and legitimate conceptions. Here again society must do what it can to provide all possible assistance to the victim including compensation (if one can speak of "compensation" in this context!) for the sacrifice she has been called upon to make. In most cases we must assume the mother will not want to keep the child after birth, at which point society's responsibility for its future development will become complete. If a mother does decide to keep her child, society will still have the obligation to make some continuing provision for adequate care and comfort.

The position I have outlined here has been described as unrealistic and even irresponsible in that it absolutizes the right of every "fertilized ovum" to develop, as one critic put it, "in a planet which can no longer support that kind of reproduction and where it threatens the possibility of realizing the lives which exist." The adjectives unrealistic and irresponsible do not trouble me; they are fairly standard descriptions of the pacifist approach, and this is a pacifist case against abortion.

What does trouble me is the rest of the criticism. The ability or inability of the planet to support present and projected population totals is still a contested issue, and even if the prospects were as desperate as the statement suggests, the question would still remain as to whether the termination of unborn life is a desirable or acceptable solution. And as for the "realization" of the life which exists, it is essential to face the prior question of who is to determine what that involves and by what standards. How long, we must ask, before the quotas now being set in terms of "zero population growth" and similar *quantitative* formulae are refined by eugenic selectionists in *qualitative* quotas instead? This is not an idle fear, and one would think that a movement dedicated to the elimination of long-standing inequalities based on the qualitative distinction of sex should be particularly sensitive to the possibility.

Beyond this there is that matter of "absolutizing" the right to life, and to this I am ready to plead guilty. At a time when moral absolutes of any kind are suspect and the fashions in theological and ethical discourse seem to have moved from situationalism to relativism and now to something approximating indifferentism, it strikes me as not only proper but imperative that we proclaim the value of every human life as well as the obligation to respect that life wherever it exists — if not for what it is at any given moment (a newly fertilized ovum; a convicted criminal; the habitual sinner) at least for what it may yet, with God's grace, become. It is not just a matter of consistency; in a very real sense it is the choice between integrity and hypocrisy. No one who publicly mourns the senseless burning of a napalmed child should be indifferent to the intentional searing of a living fetus in the womb. By the same token, the Catholic, bishop or layperson, who somehow finds it possible to maintain an olympian silence in the face of government policies which contemplate the destruction of human life on a massive scale, has no right to issue indignant protests when the same basic disregard for human life is given expression in government policies permitting or encouraging abortion.

8. The Bondage of Liberation: A Pacifist Reflection

The last thing the peace movement needs at this moment of diminished strength and influence is dissension in its dwindling ranks. The long-awaited end of the Indochina hostilities has left most of the more active opponents of that war in a state of near total exhaustion. Many have turned to the more routine pursuits necessarily neglected in those years of personal trial and disruption. The great numbers who had become part of "the peace movement" with the strictly limited objective of doing what they could to bring a speedy end to the conflict have now pulled out, leaving the broader peace concerns to the more traditional pacifist organizations and peace churches that have always carried the major part of the load. Even these, however, have encountered difficulties in their efforts to maintain the active participation of their members and supporters.

Tireless vehicles of organized peace activity such as the War Resisters League and the Fellowship of Reconciliation are hard pressed to meet even the minimal expenses of their drastically reduced programs.

Prudence, then, would counsel that this is a time to "accentuate the positive" and avoid risking any kind of split among the relative few who have not succumbed to the temptations of a retreat to normalcy and apathy. But there is another and quite contrary case to be argued. Precisely in this time of weakness it might be courting disaster for the peace movement to blind itself to a very real challenge that, if unmet and unresolved, could tear it apart and leave it helpless before the next crisis. United though the movement may be on such issues as amnesty, disarmament, and ending nuclear proliferation, there is at least the potential of disunity on another, which involves the basic, the core values of pacifism. If only to preserve its cherished integrity of purpose, this issue and its troubling implications must be brought into the open and examined.

The issue, simply put, involves the compatibility of a thorough commitment to pacifist ideals with support for national liberation movements. Theoretically, of course, there need be no problem. The values proclaimed by each may even be said to depend upon the other to some extent. At this level, to present it as a matter of choice — peace or liberation, peace *versus* liberation — is a distortion. Yet in practice it is not so easy. Any given situation may, and usually does, impose at least a sequence of temporal priority that can require the temporary sacrifice or suspension of the one to preserve or advance the prospects of the other. This is no false dilemma, and, needless to say, it is one that the religious pacifist cannot long ignore.

This is one pacifist's reflection: no definitive solution is offered. Nor should this be mistaken for a critical evaluation of what has become known as "the theology of liberation," though, obviously, that body of propositions and its applications to actual conflicts are a central concern. I am not sufficiently familiar with the scholarly production of that doctrine's proponents, and I can claim no competence in purely theological debate. As a sociologist, however, I am familiar with the applications and, as a religious pacifist, more than a little concerned about their relevance to my personal rejection of all war and violence.

The present dilemma takes its sharpest form in three crucial contexts. First and most obvious is the question of acceptable means, specifically the use or endorsement of violence. Second, and more subtle, is the process of "conscientization" and its appropriate techniques and objectives. Last, and usually ignored, is the acceptance of nationalism as a motivating force and justification.

That all of these present problems only for those who profess to be part of an authentic peace movement should be evident enough. Unfortunately, there are a goodly number of the latter who are not quite willing to take a definite stand on these questions if, as is almost certainly the case, they are required to criticize or even oppose existing movements for national liberation.

Graphic illustration of this fact was provided at a recent meeting of Pax Christi International in Montserrat which I attended as an American delegate. Our Spanish hosts, who preferred to be identified as the *Catalan* section of this Catholic peace movement, took every opportunity to promote the case for Catalonian liberation from what they viewed as the repressive government in Madrid. So urgent and persuasive were their arguments — which, to be honest, most of us were predisposed to accept anyway — that most of the participants joined briefly in a vigil outside the walls of a Barcelona prison where political prisoners were then incarcerated.

A more formal endorsement of the Catalonian position came with the passage of a set of resolutions protesting all forms of political oppression and calling for recognition of the rights of conscientious objectors. More significant, however, was what was not included. As originally presented, the resolutions included a specific condemnation of "oppressive violence." A Belgian delegate proposed the addition of the words, "from any quarter," but this drew instant opposition from the Catalans and their supporters. The amendment was approved with slight modifications, after which the original sponsors, following a brief caucus recess, moved to eliminate the entire reference to violence. The message was clear. Although they insisted they were committed to nonviolence in their own actions, they preferred to forgo any definite condemnation of violence that might be interpreted, even by implication, as criticism of other segments of the liberation movement that did not share their commitment. The motion passed.

An even more dramatic example of the intellectual tension between adherence to the cause of liberation and commitment to the ideals and methods of the peacemaker is provided by the little book, *My Life for My Friends: The Guerrilla Journal of Nestor Paz, Christian* (Orbis 1975). This is the account of one young man's total commitment to a cause he had decided could be achieved only by violence, "the only path left open to us, painful as it may be." It would be superficial and unjust to dismiss this document as the work of an unfeeling extremist, indifferent to the death and destruction he might bring; just as it is superficial and unjust to dismiss, as Paz does, the pacifist as indifferent to the sufferings of the oppressed.

It is a short and tragic story. Less than three months after leaving home to join the guerrilla band Paz would die of starvation. He was perhaps as much the victim of those he wished to liberate but who failed to provide him and his companions with the support and sustenance they needed. The real tragedy goes beyond the sacrifice of a gifted young poet, former seminarian, and teacher of religion. The tragedy is to be found in the rationale that led him to his fate, a sadly confused mixture of ideological themes drawn in almost equal parts from the New Testament and revolutionary Marxist rhetoric. If he applied to himself the "no greater love" teaching of the Gospel to legitimate the course he had chosen, this did not detract from his approval of the oath-taking ceremony "before a picture of Che Guevara." The important distinction between laying down one's life for a cause and setting forth to destroy the lives of others for that same cause seems not to have occurred to him. Indeed, at one point he goes so far as to suggest the martyrdom of St. Stephen reported in Acts as a spiritual parallel to the violent resistance in which he was engaged.

One objection to "liberation theology" as popularly interpreted and applied is that it restores to respectability the "just war" morality that had become so thoroughly discredited by the excesses of World War II and, more recently, by Vietnam. Worse still, by effectively reducing the traditional criteria for such a "just war" to only two (just cause and right intention, both generously interpreted) it has opened the way to virtually uncritical support not only for wars of national liberation but for the full range of guerrilla tactics, not excluding indiscriminate acts of terrorism. Criteria such as proportionality, justice of the means, prospects of success, and others are either ignored or dismissed as secondary considerations. Thus, active resistance to oppression, certainly a "just cause" in an almost tautological sense, and the "right intention" — expressed by Nestor Paz as "to defend the unlettered and undernourished majority from the exploitation of a minority and to win back dignity for a dehumanized people" — are deemed sufficient in themselves to cover the proverbial "multitude of sins."

The problem, for the Christian pacifist at least, centers upon whether such laudable objectives are to be, or even *can* be, achieved through violence. It is a question deserving a more serious answer than the easy play on words represented by the argument that the violence of the guerrilla warrior should not be considered as violence but, rather, as *counter*violence, a forced response to the violence perpetrated by the status quo. As a sociologist I would be the last to deny the reality of "systemic violence," but as a Christian I must recognize an obligation to do what I can to reduce or eliminate violence of any kind. The counterviolence of Nestor Paz and his friends is as incompatible with the lessons and spirit of the Gospel as are the injustices that inspired him to take up arms in the first place.

The retributive counterviolence promoted by the popular interpretations of liberation theology goes beyond "just war" thinking to adopt an approximation of the "*total* war" perspective. Guerrilla and terrorist actions are keyed not only to reprisal actions against officials responsible for repressive policies but extend, almost inevitably, to anyone guilty of "supporting the system," no matter how indirect the support may be. From the culpable official to the obedient policeman (and his family) the defined target broadens to include the minor clerk in some government bureaucracy, the conscientious taxpayer, and, sooner or later, those members of the oppressed classes who may not be ready, or sufficiently eager, to join the forces of liberation. It may well be that guerrilla warfare by its very nature cannot be expected to respect the distinctions and restraints that, in theory at least, govern conventional war. If so, instead of justifying the extremes of conduct that some are willing to accept, this should be one more reason for the convinced Christian *not* to approve or participate.

It is at this point that "conscientization" becomes directly relevant to the discussion. Too often those who are willing to encourage and even promote violent opposition to repressive regimes will be equally insistent that "outsiders" have no right to speak to the victims of oppression about nonviolent alternatives.

Conscientization — that awkward term referring to the process for raising political consciousness and awakening in the victim an awareness of his dignity and rights as a human person — too easily becomes one of imposing elitist definitions and aspirations upon "the common man" without giving due consideration to the additional burdens and sacrifices he might have to bear as a result.

The fact that Nestor Paz was the son of a Bolivian general and provincial governor and enjoyed all the educational advantages and privileges associated with membership in the ruling class clearly enhances the sacrifice he was ready to make for the cause of justice. At the same time, however, we must not overlook the fact that this same background provided him with a perspective and a set of values different in many important respects from those shared by the victims of social injustice. Out of this difference would come the note of "Marxist elitism" that surfaces from time to time in his journal entries. On the eve of the battle that would bring a disastrous defeat he writes: "We are being purified. Combat will purge us even more. *Out of this experience that select group will be drawn which will bring the people to the happiness they so rightly deserve.* This is the result of a long and constant faithfulness to the revolutionary ideal incarnated in the life of the guerrilla." (The emphasis is mine; the elitist implications, his.) It is Paz and his guerrilla companions who know the score, who are or will provide "the select few" to "bring" the people to the happiness they "deserve." The tragic fact that "the people" would prove unready to accept, or even support, what Paz and his companions defined as the means to their "happiness" spelled his ultimate defeat and death.

It should not be too difficult to understand. The victims of exploitation will always define happiness in more modest terms than a person of Paz's privileged background could understand or would be likely to approve. Sociologists make much of the concept, "relative deprivation," noting that revolutions do not often originate with the utterly destitute and helpless. Instead, the inspired leadership and lasting power will come from those individuals who, though comparatively well off, regard themselves as not as well off as they ought to be. The true prisoners of starvation and wretched of the earth are likely to place too great a value on today's crust of bread and the rags they wear to risk that slight difference promised by the middle- or upper-class revolutionary. As far as they are concerned, it is not only the advocate of pious resignation to their unhappy lot who offers them pie in the sky.

Conscientization, quite properly, aims at creating the sense of relative deprivation where it should, but does not yet, exist. To the extent that it succeeds, it almost certainly involves the risk to the victim of what little he has by inviting the wrath and the reprisals of the guardians of the status quo. The would-be "liberator" must take this into account, recognizing that one result of his efforts will be to add to the burden of oppression already endured by those he would free. And when, as too often happens, guerrilla actions are directed against the already helpless and exploited in order to force them to some measure of compliance, the cause of justice is as likely to be betrayed as served by the violence employed.

Passive resignation is not the only, nor even an acceptable, alternative. The ardent advocate of peace, like his militant liberationist counterpart, recognizes the need for an effective program of conscientization. What differences there are — and they are crucial — are differences of approach and emphasis, not of objective. For one thing, the religious pacifist should find it difficult if not altogether impossible to embrace the deterministic implications of Marxist rhetoric and its solutions cast entirely in terms of "creating structures" that will "make" men brothers. The sense of inherent human dignity and the inspiration to strive toward the fulfillment of one's true potential are not likely to be served by theories or programs that define the individual and his rights entirely in terms of the place he occupies in the social and political order. No one can be indifferent to the importance of considerations such as existing class differences and the inequities of the maldistribution of wealth and opportunity associated with those differences in social rank. But the solution is not to be found in a model of egalitarian collective in which all individuality is either suppressed or restricted to whatever limits may be permitted by some dictatorial authority or consensus. No matter how much "better off" the human "units" may be when measured by standards of material well-being, the citizen-as-cog, however acquiescent the cog and smooth functioning the societal machine, is incompatible with the Christian vision of the just society.

The thoroughly justifiable effort to arouse an awareness of deprivation where such awareness was lacking need not become the occasion for deliberately inciting a spirit of animosity and hatred. The thirst for justice should never be reduced to the thirst for the oppressor's blood. If Nestor Paz had given more profound reflection to his choice of St. Stephen as a guerrilla model, he could scarcely have missed the point that Stephen had been obedient to *his model,* Christ, and prayed for his oppressors even as they were stoning him to death. None of what Paz calls the "deeds of liberation" recorded in the New Testament support his conclusion, sincere though it undoubtedly was, that "taking up arms is the only way of protecting the poor against their present exploitation, the only way of generating a free man."

To the extent that the hatreds incited by revolutionary "conscientization" are directed against categories (the "ruling classes," "imperialists" — and, of course, their "lackeys"), it follows that the "retribution" meted out is similarly categorical in nature. One need not repeat the grim litany of terrorist atrocities perpetrated in the name of liberation over the past several years. It is important to note, however, that these have not always received the condemnation or even criticism they deserved from more liberal-minded advocates of peace. Instead, a kind of double standard exists that permits too many of the latter to maintain silence in the face of actions which, had they been committed by what Paz refers to as the "gorilla soldiers" of the government forces, would have provoked immediate and unequivocal denunciation (which, of course, they would have deserved).

Consciousness *must* be raised, but the objective must be the conscientization of victim and oppressor alike so that each will come to recognize and respect the humanity of the other as the only true measure of the humanity in themselves. Just as the one must be instructed in the obligations of love and justice, the other must be instructed in the practice of love and forgiveness.

The difficulty of this process is intensified by the intrusion of nationalism as a major factor in the liberation movements and their appeal. Already in the period between the two world wars, nationalism was described as "the characteristic heresy of our day," and there is little that has happened since to discredit that judgment. The linkage between nationalism and liberation may be easy enough to understand. That so many individuals ostensibly committed to peace should accept and even approve that linkage is not.

It would be foolish to deny that peoples moving toward liberation — in Africa, Asia, Latin America — will seek to establish a national identity as the culminating step in removing the last vestiges of political and economic imperialism.

Whether in doing so they must recapitulate the sorry history that has bloodied the continents of Europe and North America is quite another matter. Unfortunately, too many assume that is the case, that a turn toward nationalism with its exclusivist prides and rivalries is a "natural stage," something like adolescence, through which the newly liberated colonies must pass if they are to reach full independence and maturity. And as they insist upon erecting the barriers that will separate them from other peoples with whom they so recently shared a common subjection, every new nation finds it necessary to expend enormous energies and funds in defending those barriers. This, in turn, requires a concentration of governmental power — often enough in the hands of the military leaders entrusted with that defense — and the all-too-frequent result is that "liberation" ends up as little more than an exchange of one oppression for another.

European movements for national liberation reverse the direction but not the process. Here the objective is simply one of restoring old national identities that have been lost or suppressed, usually as the result of military defeat. "Underground" movements abound in the former Baltic states (Lithuania, Latvia, Estonia), in the Balkan remnant populations, and in the other Eastern bloc nations that, though theoretically autonomous, exist largely at the pleasure of the Soviet Union. All these movements draw inspiration from the residues of traditions and hallowed customs celebrating remembered glories and accomplishments. It might even be argued that, since these populations are subject to persecution aimed at crushing those lingering echoes of nationhood, they can claim a greater measure of legitimacy for their struggle than can the emerging nations of the Third World with no similar historical supports for their cause.

It would be pointless to press that distinction, however. The sacrifices being made by those who, on the one hand, seek to recover and, on the other, to establish a national identity deserve respect and admiration. At the same time, the insistence upon unrestricted self-determination once that identity is achieved constitutes a distinct threat to the just and enduring peace that is the only hope of survival for humankind. What the world most urgently needs is less nationalism, not more. In the shadow of the mushroom cloud we can no longer afford the dangerous illusions that, if one accepts Gil Eliot's estimates in his *Twentieth Century Book of the Dead,* have already cost more than a hundred million lives since this century began. Perhaps nothing demonstrates the insidious nature of nationalism better than the tragic degeneration of the United Nations from the vehicle of international cooperation and understanding its founders intended to what it has become today, a noisy arena of confrontation between spokespersons for selfish national interests.

Instead of supporting further proliferation of separate and sovereign nations, the peace movement should be marshaling its influence to reduce and ultimately eliminate nationalism as a divisive force in human affairs. Although the principle has always been central to its program in the past, it has never been more crucial than it is today. *All* of the major threats to human survival — not only war and its promise of nuclear annihilation, but other issues such as the pollution of the atmosphere and the seas, famine and disease, the inequitable distribution of diminishing world resources — are clearly beyond the capacity of any single state or even regional combinations of states to resolve. On another front, the emergence of great multinational corporations and their rapidly escalating domination over the world economy have made a mockery of presumably "sacred" boundaries and pretensions to any meaningful degree of sovereign authority or national self-determination.

It should be eminently clear to anyone committed to the cause of world peace that a further fractioning of the globe and its inhabitants is an invitation to disaster, that some alternative must be found to a world order based upon the costly factions of supreme state sovereignty, self-defined national interest, balance-of-power diplomacy, and the like. One such alternative is the vision of a pluralist world order keyed to a commonality of interests, one that would recognize and respect differences in identities — be they racial, religious, class, or whatever — while acknowledging that these are secondary to the essential identity of all men and women as members of a single, and endangered, species.

Such a vision will be dismissed as "impractical" and "too idealistic" of course. These dismissive criticisms have always been applied to the peace movement; far from being an embarrassment, they should be regarded as a compliment, a source of pride. A peace movement that is "too idealistic" might better serve the cause of human liberation than the cold, harsh pragmatics that seem now to dominate movements directed toward the liberationalist ideal. If revolution be the objective, it might as well be the total revolution that could really change the world by rejecting *both* the vehicle of oppression, the all-powerful national state, and its ultimate claim to power: violence.

The issue, then, is not a choice between peace and liberation (or between peace and justice) as some believe. If we agree that without justice there can be no true or lasting peace, an equally strong case can be made that the "justice" to be gained at the cost of wholesale death and destruction through war or violent revolution is neither certain nor, as too much recent history shows, likely to be of long duration. The crusade to liberate the world from the threat of fascist domination ended with half of Europe subject to Soviet domination instead. More ominously, it ended with the liberators converted to Hitler's infamous doctrine of total war. Since then, costly struggles to overthrow imperialist or rightist oppression (in Cuba, Vietnam, Cambodia, to cite but a few examples) seem to have produced new oppressions from the other extreme of the political spectrum. The old Scholastic maxim has relevance here: the means usually do turn out to be the end "in the process of becoming."

The brutality and torture applied today by the military juntas in Chile, Thailand, and far too many other places deserve universal condemnation. Whether the situation is improved by brutality and torture at the hands of would-be liberators — which, in turn, are used to "justify" more brutality and torture at the hands of the oppressors — is not at all certain. At some point the vicious circle must be broken. A good beginning, perhaps, would be for all who are interested in peace and liberation to develop more objective standards of protest.

Such standards would inspire the same measure of protest against restrictive policies of post-liberation Vietnam that drive Buddhist monks to acts of self-immolation as once marked the protest in response to similar acts directed against Diem and his successors.

Nestor Paz, I fear, would have little patience with such a proposition. As he saw it, people like myself who speak of nonviolence, peace, and the Gospel instead of joining him and his comrades-in-arms are "today's Pharisees." If his criticism has any validity, it lies in the degree to which the pacifist fails to accept a personal responsibility to oppose policies and programs that maintain the injustices Paz set out to fight. It is important, therefore, that we demand of our leaders and policymakers that financial support be withheld from any regime — whether of the Right, like Chile, or of the Left, like the USSR — which does not respect the basic human rights of its subjects. We must insist upon an immediate termination of programs for the training of police or security forces, including our own, which include instruction in the arts of torture or which are clearly designed to suppress legitimate expression of dissent. In a more positive vein, economic policies should be developed and advanced that would favor international cooperation, produce an equitable distribution of the world's resources, and restrict the exploitive operations of the multinational corporations.

Finally, when violence does erupt within populations reaching out toward freedom, we should stand ready to provide the funds and facilities that will be needed to relieve the hardships suffered by those innocently caught up in the struggle. The refusal to support or condone violence does not require that we maintain a detached or neutral attitude. Even though we do not take an active part, we can and should open our gates and once again become the safe haven for refugees and other victims of the struggle against oppression.

How we as individuals can best contribute to these ends is something each of us must determine. Many will choose the course of activist, though nonviolent, confrontation, while others prefer the less disruptive approach of intellectual persuasion and political activity. Some, assuming the phrase has not lost its meaning for contemporary Christians, will find the answer in the "weapons of the Spirit" and try to advance the twin causes of peace and justice through works of penance and prayer.

A Nestor Paz would probably be dissatisfied by this, as will others who accept his thesis that liberation can come only through violent conflict. But one should be able to hope that those who see themselves as part of a peace movement and who have worked in the past to oppose or reject war as a solution to human problems or as an instrument for achieving justice will be more open to the arguments presented here. It is the old story of not following false prophets with their overly simple solutions. Christ the Liberator is not likely to be found behind the guerrilla's rifle or planting the terrorist's bomb in some crowded marketplace. He is certain to be found where He has always promised to be: in the hearts of those willing to love their enemies and, if need be, to suffer injustice and even death in His Name rather than return evil for evil.

9.
In Our Image

Juvenile delinquency is not a new phenomenon. In the "old days" (c. 1910 and World War I) "Teutonia Indians" and "Bloody Sixty-six" stirred much the same chill of terror now evoked by "Cobras," "Silver Arrows," and the other colorful names chosen by the marauding gangs of today. Then, as now, national-origin and racial loyalties and prejudices combined with common area of residence to unite individual toughs into a predatory force — though the "territory" was then more an area of identification than a realm subject to the absolute sovereignty of a street gang.

But the similarities soon fade away before the differences between the gangs of then and now. The misdeeds of the earlier delinquents, as they are remembered at least, seemed to consist of such offenses as crashing private parties for the purpose of carrying off whatever edibles and potables might be found. Acts of physical violence generally involved clashes with those who tried to interfere or resist these forays. This is not to say, of course, that they never engaged in more serious offences, but at least they were not known for them.

The escapades our elders recall would be regarded today as innocent pranks when compared with the terror that rules the streets of a modern metropolis.

The gang delinquents of our day boast of arsenals that include broken bottles, tire irons, knives, assault guns, dynamite, and acid. They are better organized and far more numerous. Their delinquencies are marked by greater daring and viciousness. Instead of being occasional and unexpected, their activities have come to be regarded as commonplace, even routine, occurrences. All generations have their share of sadists and compulsive killers, but organized beatings and killings "just for kicks," as described, for instance, by Harrison Salisbury (*The Shook-up Generation*) seem to indicate a new trend. This is especially compelling when considered in the light of the most horrifying fact of all — the steady decline in the age levels at which these offenses are committed.

Journalists, novelists, psychologists, and sociologists have all concerned themselves with the shook-up generation, its problems, and its frightening behavior in the hope of discovering the reason and a cure for juvenile delinquency. For the most part the journalists and the novelists have had the greater impact. Salisbury, Benjamin Fine, and their many colleagues can draw upon the full sensationalism of the problem in all its lurid dimensions to shock the public into awareness. Their more literary brothers probe into the inner depths of Nick Romano, Tomboy, and the Amboy Dukes to play upon the sensitivities and sympathies of the understanding reader. Both approaches, however, rest upon the oversimplification of a complex problem, and it is no surprise to find the explanation (and the solution) expressed in similarly oversimplified form — whether it stresses family responsibility and laxity, the hereditary determinism of "a bad seed," or the environmental determinism that assures the reader that the delinquent lurks behind any door in any slum neighborhood.

One would like to be able to say that the social scientist has done much better, but, generally speaking, he has not. True, we have a wealth of carefully detailed and large-scale research programs furnishing clear evidence of the multi-dimensional character of the delinquency problem, but as these seldom reach the general public, most people hear and accept the more superficial explanations. And even if the scientific studies were known, it is unlikely that they would be effective, for the more careful the method and the broader the scope of such investigation, the less likely it is to produce conclusions that lend themselves to general explanations and applications. The net result is that while social scientists have been able to free themselves from the easy attraction of deterministic explanations, the layman becomes ever more impatient with the growing complexity of their findings and ever more willing to turn to the daily newspaper or the latest paperback for the real, down-to-earth facts and answers.

This is not to say that the social scientist has contributed nothing. He has helped to establish some degree of validity, however limited, to most of the "common sense" explanations. There are now studies which give clear statistical support to the harmful influence of a bad physical environment, to the destructive impact of a broken home; and detailed case history analysis has confirmed the role played by the individual's own physiological and psychological malformation or maladjustments. To the extent that all the "total" explanations are given scientific support, however, they necessarily suffer some deflation and modification.

These findings represent important gains, of course, but they offer small consolation when we compare them with the rate of increase in the incidence and malevolence of the phenomenon itself. The evil is fast outdistancing our poor efforts to isolate its causes, much less cure or even control it.

Perhaps this is because we are looking for the wrong kind of cause — or looking in the wrong places. The study of the delinquent, juvenile or adult, is usually set in the framework of a deviation from the accepted social norms; he is seen as a rebel with or without a cause who, alone or in the company of other like-minded rebels, scorns and seeks to overthrow the dominant values of society. Occasionally one encounters an exception — Albert K. Cohen's 1955 study (*Delinquent Boys: The Culture of the Gang*) being one outstanding example — which approaches the delinquency problem as one not of deviation in itself but, rather, of conformity to a deviant value system held by some group more immediately crucial to the delinquent than the more abstract and distant society. This is an important shift of focus: neither the individual nor even the gang but, instead, the subculture of the neighborhood or community becomes the culprit.

This should not be confused with the old-style environmental determinism which viewed delinquency as the direct product of material deprivation, slum housing, recreational deficiencies, etc. These things are important, of course, but they are now seen as important through their contribution to a cultural setting in which distinctive patterns of social interaction emerge producing an equally distinctive systems of values. Such values can linger on long after the tenement gives way to the public housing towers and their carefully planned playground facilities and programs. It is in the molding force of such subcultures that one may find the best leads to an understanding of the problem of the delinquent and his behavior.

Though this approach does emphasize the conformity aspect of delinquency, it still holds to the basic deviation formula, merely shifting the onus of the delinquency to the deviant neighborhood subculture. As such it would apply to the Teutonia Indians of the 1910s, to the Egyptian Kings of the 1950s, and to their counterparts today. We are still left with the problem of the critical differences between them. To understand these an even more dramatic approach may be in order, one which departs from the basic deviation concept as it is customarily employed.

No one would suggest that the behavior patterns we call delinquency are not a serious departure from the general norms (at least as the general norms are expressed). However, though the fact of deviation is accepted, one may still challenge the direction usually ascribed to that deviation. I am suggesting here that the present delinquency problem — certainly its most significant characteristics — represent not a rejection or flouting of our contemporary social values as is usually taken for granted but, instead, an over-acceptance of those values producing a distortion in the form of carrying them to their logical extremes.

The key to this admittedly shocking hypothesis lies in the quality, not quantity, of delinquent behavior. Its prevailing characteristics tend to incorporate, first, an utter disregard of the intrinsic worth of human life and rights; second, an almost completely hedonistic orientation abandoning or denying all moral self-restraint; and, third, a slavish acceptance of peer group evaluations as the final test of one's own importance and meaning to himself.

It should not be too difficult to see that these characteristics are really exaggerations of behavior guides that govern normal and respectable ways of life. The joy-riding young demons on a hundred-mile-an-hour spree in a stolen car are not too far removed from the reputable exurbanite heedlessly pushing his chariot of death to its maximum speed — or, for that matter, from the equally reputable manufacturer who was well aware that his product's greater size and increased speed would be measured by record highs in highway murder.

The alcohol-drug-and-sex orgy of the teenage gang finds striking parallels at a more restrained level in the mores and tastes of enlightened sophisticated society and are certainly a direct response — perhaps more honest, however crude, to the battery of sex-and-fun stimuli to which all of us are subjected by the advertiser, the sensationalist press, and the prominent figures of the entertainment world.

Finally, the importance of proving oneself to his fellows, even though proof that one is not "chicken" may involve some act of delinquency, mirrors grotesquely the unending striving for status and acceptance, regardless of the price, that sets and maintains the pace in the rat-race of the organization man.

If this is the shook-up generation, that term applies to us all, not only to the teenage thug with the assault gun and the leather jacket. Whence our right to criticize his disregard for human life, we who have seen the bodies burned to ashes at Buchenwald and Hiroshima, we who are willing to accept the fact that we are preparing to use ("only as a last resort," of course) new and inhumanly murderous weapons that are on target if they fall within 50 miles of their military objective? How can we who have renounced our own sense of ultimate personal moral responsibility challenge the conformity of the youth who rides the social current into the jungle of the street gang? It is no accident that the most vicious gangs model their organization, their alliances, and their rumbles after the patterns set for them by their highly respected elders who engage in the game of international power politics.

Fortunately not all of us carry our social values to such logical extremes of violence, and it is here that specific personal or social handicaps and influences become relevant as selective factors. Most of us, juveniles and adults, do manage to develop a measure of self-restraint and maturity that makes it possible to draw lines and call a halt this side of delinquency and crime. Not so the delinquent. Limited intellectual endowment or retarded intellectual development, poor home and neighborhood environments, economic and recreational deprivation — all these familiar "causal" factors serve to make him more susceptible to the underlying but pervasive amorality or outright immorality of the general culture. Just as inferior physical endowment and development or a state of physical weakness makes some individuals more readily susceptible than others to infection when all are equally exposed to a raging epidemic.

Salisbury comes close to this conclusion by declaring in his book that "surely it is in our value system that the germ of the trouble lies hidden." Even more to the point are the words of Albert Schweitzer he quotes: "Increasingly there is lost the consciousness that every man is an object of concern for us just because he is a man; civilization and morals are shaken and the advance to fully developed inhumanity is only a question of time."

Is this the factor that has been lacking to confound all our efforts to explain and solve the problem of the delinquent — the patterned inhumanity of society itself, arising from the loss of any sense of individual human dignity and moral responsibility? If so, it is futile for us to turn to such proposals as a "return to the woodshed" penology or the more elaborate but equally sterile blueprints of the social engineer. The real solution becomes terribly simple, just as it is terribly hard. Man must again become an object of concern for us "just because he is a man" and not because he is a potential customer or competitor, fellow national or enemy, or even the anonymous "other" who has it in his power to help or hinder us in our efforts to find a comfortable niche in an admittedly uncomfortable world.

The horror that stalks our streets has been fashioned in our image, not an image buried in the night depths of subconscious fears and evil urges, but an image blazoned forth in headlines, on billboards, everywhere we turn. Until we correct our value system (the one we live by, not the one we proclaim), until we destroy the deadly germ from which the poison growth of delinquency has sprung, it is a hopeless challenge that we face.

10.
Memories of Warner

One of the signs of advancing age is the tendency to attach extra importance to anniversaries of past events, especially those in which one was personally involved. Some anniversaries, it goes without saying, are more important than others. Occasionally there will be one which, because the event itself was small in scale, will seem unimportant but nevertheless should not go unmarked. One such will take place this October (1992), the 50th anniversary of the opening of the Civilian Public Service camp at Warner, N.H., operated under the auspices of the Association of Catholic Conscientious Objectors. For those who never heard of the ACCO — and this will probably include most of today's readers — it is perhaps best described as the World War II Catholic Worker pacifist "front" organization.

Historical purists will argue that the more significant event was the opening of Warner's predecessor camp at Stoddard, N.H., in June 1941. Perhaps so. The justification for giving Warner special attention (apart from the fact that it was the camp to which I was assigned, my arrival coinciding nicely with the camp's official opening) is that Warner is where the largest number of Catholic CO's came together and where the real "character" of the Catholic CPS experience emerged most clearly.

That "largest group," it is well to note, was not very large. Altogether only 75 men were assigned to Warner during its brief (five months) existence, and there were probably no more than 50 or 60 on its roster at any one time. This was a far cry indeed from the hundreds so confidently anticipated by the people at the Mott Street "headquarters" of the ACCO at the time they succeeded in overriding Dorothy Day's objections to involving the CW in the administration of a conscription program.

Small as the total was, it was more impressive than the Stoddard beginnings. That camp was on the verge of never being opened by Selective Service because there were not enough (Catholic) assignees to justify a work project. It was saved by a desperate recruitment effort among other nearby CPS camps to persuade enough men to volunteer for transfer to the imperiled Catholic camp. The eight transfers thus obtained made it possible for Stoddard to receive official status on October 6, 1941. A year later the move to larger — and, it was hoped, more viable — facilities marked the beginning of the Warner experience.

Though this was the first "corporate" witness against an ongoing war on the part of Catholics (a mere handful of Catholics, to be sure), it went unacknowledged and unsupported by the rest of the Church. Even so, its history stands in sharp contrast to the almost total absence of Catholic opposition to World War I on the one hand and the "great Catholic peace conspiracy" of the Berrigans and others against the war in Vietnam on the other.

It would be gratifying to be able to claim a causal linkage to the three, but that would be claiming too much. Perhaps the most that can be said with any certainty is that the World War II "witness" served as a kind of precedent. No longer could draft authorities maintain that Catholics cannot be conscientious objectors; more important, no longer did Catholics opposed to war feel, as most of the Warner men must have felt at times, that there was nothing in Catholic tradition or history to justify their refusal.

It was quite appropriate that the beginnings of Camp Simon, the name chosen by the campers at Stoddard and continued at Warner, depended on non-Catholic volunteers, for a religious mixture was to be the dominant characteristic of the camp's history. In my research I was surprised to discover that 50 of the 75 men assigned to Warner were Catholic; my impression at the time, recorded in letters written to friends, would have placed no more than half in that category. The difference was traceable to the fact that a number of men identified as such in Selective Service records were what, in those less enlightened days, would be referred to as "fallen-away" (non-practicing) Catholics. But even if we accept the 50 as the records identify them, the question would still remain: how to account that fully one-third of the camp membership of the only *Catholic* camp were not of that religious persuasion?

It would be nice to say that this religious breakdown was the result of choice, thereby making Warner as much a pioneer venture in ecumenism as it was with respect to conscientious objection. This would be true only in part and even then quite by accident. Actually, the mixture of faiths was again due to the failure of the ACCO to produce enough Catholic objectors to meet the work project requirements. To fill the vacuum Selective Service assigned men who were not Catholic but who did not fit into the other religious categories with camps of their own (Friends, Mennonites, and Brethren).

And what a mixture it was! Among the non-Catholic element were men who claimed other, but still traditional, religious affiliations. Two of these became regular participants in the most consciously Catholic "chapel group" and reliable supporters of the Catholic Worker camp administration. It was a somewhat different matter for others who openly proclaimed themselves as atheists or agnostics and tended to be, if not disruptively rebellious (some were), at least wary of being subjected to Catholic practices or standards and CW principles of voluntary poverty. Technically these men should have been ineligible for Civilian Public Service status since the law restricted the IV-E (conscientious objector) classification to those who "by reason of religious training and belief" were opposed to all war. Draft board ignorance of that restriction may account for their being there or, a more likely explanation, a prudential decision that sending potential troublemakers to an isolated forestry camp in the New Hampshire woods was a convenient solution to what otherwise might have been a community problem.

Strictly speaking, of course, the Catholics had no right to be there either. Under traditional "just war/unjust war" teachings it could be argued that opposition to all wars was excluded as an option for them. The relatively few Catholics who did take a frankly pacifist stand would have been hard pressed to prove they did so as a result of their "religious training." Even the CW contingent, which was willing to allow for the possibility of the "just war" but held that the Christian seeking perfection should go beyond justice, would find it difficult to pass the legalistic test. Then there was the final group, the source of some of the liveliest camp debates, consisting of followers of Fr. Coughlin; some of them based their objection to military service on the grounds that, as they saw it, the United States was fighting on the wrong side. Had the nation joined forces with the Axis opponents of Bolshevism, so their argument went, no Catholic could legitimately claim to be a conscientious objector! These differences of interpretation among the Catholics — with the adherents of each position maintaining its correctness and rejecting the others as error — created more dissension in camp than the differences between Catholic and non-Catholic.

Readers of the monthly column in the *Catholic Worker* reporting on events at Warner learned nothing of these divisions. Instead they were given an over-idealized picture of a community united in a spirit of wholehearted sacrifice and joint effort. Only rarely (and then only those "in the know" would be able to read between the lines) was there any hint of the real situation. There were perfectly good reasons for this reticence, over and above the camp administration's (largely CWs in background and sympathy) inclination to turn the other cheek. These monthly reports were the only vehicle for appealing for material support for the camp and its members. To have presented a more accurate description would have sullied the image of the conscientious objector as hero and decreased the prospects of a generous response.

And make no mistake, those appeals were absolutely essential to survival. The fact that the camp ultimately did not survive was due to the ACCO's inability to maintain even minimal standards of diet and physical care. This was not, as some of the more severe critics charged, an intentional "imposition" by the CW administration of the movement's principles and ideology, though it *was* true that the camp's standard of living was comparable to that prevailing at the CW's Houses of Hospitality on the Bowery and the "skid rows" of other cities. The explanation was simple enough: whatever funds were available for Warner came from the same limited sources that supported the rest of the CW works of spiritual and corporal mercy.

At Stoddard, the grand vision had seen campers returning from their day's work "on project" and devoting free time to cultivating a subsistence farm — both a CW-type ideal and, more practically, the only hope of ensuring sufficient food. It did not work out that way. Except for raising some pigs as a meat supply (with dubious results) and a more successful venture in caring for a flock of chickens, that grand vision soon faded before the harsh realities of New Hampshire weather and the general lack of dedication (or principled refusal to cooperate) on the part of the campers.

That principled refusal was directed more against the CPS program itself than against the camp administration. All of the men who had applied for the IV-E classification in effect "requested" assignment to alternate service. Still it would be wrong to regard this as a truly voluntary choice since the only other available options were either the military service to which they were opposed in conscience or prison. Forced into making that choice, many felt it was reasonable to expect the government which had conscripted them into service to provide them with the essentials of food, work clothing, and shelter as well as compensation comparable to that received by men conscripted into the "other" services. That none of these expectations was fulfilled was due to the arrangement made by the three major "peace" churches under which religious sponsoring agencies assumed responsibility for the actual operation of the Civilian Public Service program. The ACCO became an astonishing fourth among the initial sponsors without being able to match the others in terms of resources for undertaking such responsibility.

The peace church agencies could count on supportive church membership and adequate budgets, whereas the ACCO depended entirely upon the contributions made by readers and friends of its CW parent. Subjected to an inadequate diet and other deprivations, the men of Stoddard-Warner regarded themselves as doubly victimized. Some recognition of their almost desperate state may be seen in the practice of men in other camps forgoing meals so the funds thus saved might be helped to meet Warner needs. Needless to say, this was not enough. It was this inability to meet subsistence standards more than anything else that led Selective Service to decide to close the camp in March 1943 and transfer most of its members to camps and special units operated by the Society of Friends.

The lack of pay was an issue beyond the competence of the religious sponsor agencies to resolve, even had they wished to do so (which, incidentally, some did not, preferring to see that as a "second mile" sacrifice and evidence of sincerity).

That was, in fact, part of the original plan under which it was expected that men called into service would contribute $35 a month for their own support! This might have fit into the projected peacetime program with a limited term of service, but once war came and that term of service was extended to "the duration plus six months" that added touch of "voluntary" sacrifice became an insuperable hardship for men who had no supportive religious community behind them. The ACCO could not even meet the $5 monthly allowance available to men in camps under peace church administration.

It is entirely possible that all these things — the inadequate diet and other deprivations, even the lack of pay — could have been surmounted if the men could have believed they were engaged in worthwhile service. Unfortunately, however well-intentioned the peace church leaders who made the arrangements may have been, it did not take long for those assigned to the program to realize it and its idealistic promises were something of a fraud. Most of the "special service" units and perhaps some of the camp projects may have made contributions of immediate and lasting value. Judging by the Warner experience the stated purpose, "work of national importance under civilian direction," was betrayed on both counts.

Technically again, it is true the program was "civilian directed" in the sense that the camps and units were administered by the religious agencies through their National Service Board for Religious Objectors and the actual project work was administered by civilian government agencies (for Warner, the Forestry Service) to which the camps were assigned. In actuality, every policy decision of any importance was made, or had to be approved, by the military officers in charge of the Selective Service System. The guiding principle was spelled out by the director, General Hershey, in testimony at a Congressional hearing when he expressed the opinion that the conscientious objector was handled best if no one heard of him.

Selective Service's fetish for isolation and complete control put a premium on what some campers described as work of national *unimportance*. Certainly that description fit many, if not most, camp projects. Detached service assignments (medical experiments and research units, relief training, etc.) and special units (in general or mental hospitals) were regarded as important work; but the assignee fortunate enough to be sent to one of them was aware that any behavior which seemed to threaten the "Hershey principle" risked the penalty of a speedy return to the camp situation with all its frustrations.

Warner's "work of national importance" was a forestry project designed to clear timber damaged in the great New England hurricane of several years before. Men with college degrees were assigned to cleaning up the New Hampshire forest while schools were closed or understaffed for want of teachers. The contrast was not conducive to high morale in any event, and when this was combined with the severe winter, the inadequate diet, to say nothing of the general incompetence of these unwilling city-bred "woodsmen," the results were at once farcical and tragic. Malingering became an art; much of the workday "on project" was devoted to intellectual or religious debate and personal pursuits. The artists wandered off to sketch while the less talented settled for a place to stretch out and nap. The traditional cry of "Timber!" was converted into a warning that one of the government foremen was in the vicinity and a signal for earnest work activity that would subside as soon as he was again out of sight. Moreover, as the crude statistics reveal, the malingering (often, again, a "principled" malingering and protest "slowdown") on project was not the only evidence of the unimportance of the work produced. Of the 8,500 man-days of "civilian public service" performed by Warner camp, less than 1,500 were actually spent on project.

It follows that the area of the forest cleared and the work production measure in cordage actually cut and stacked was slight indeed. That too, as everyone soon realized, made little difference. As it turned out, most of what was cut and stacked was left to rot away when the camp was closed. It was enough that these objectors were kept safely isolated where no one would hear of them.

Warner might well serve as the classic example that exaggerated all the failings inherent in the CPS program, another good reason for putting its history "on the record." The state of utter destitution and deprivation which finally forced Selective Service to close the camp (and, by so doing, terminate ACCO participation in the camp phase of CPS operations) were merely added aggravations to the unimportance of the work assigned to them and the recognition that their "witness" was subject to the complete control of military officers.

Catholics in CPS were triply alienated. Like all of the men in alternative service they had alienated themselves from the rest of the war-supporting public including, in far too many instances, close friends and family. Unlike the majority of their fellow CO's, however, they were alienated as well from their Church, knowing their stand was neither supported nor approved by their spiritual leaders and fellow communicants. Indeed, though the report has been disputed, there is evidence that Selective Service had reason to believe that the Bishop of Manchester objected to having the Catholic camp in his diocese, an additional reason (as if one were needed!) for closing it. Finally, as "outsiders" in a program keyed to peace church values and standards, they felt alienated from CPS itself and subjected to what they scathingly resented as "second-miler" and "200-percenter" philosophies and objectives imposed upon them by the (Protestant) pacifist leadership without their consent and approval.

When Warner closed most of the men were transferred to a Friends' camp in Maryland which also closed a few months later. At that time part of the Warner remnant transferred to form a special unit (again under ACCO direction) at the Rosewood State Training School for the retarded near Baltimore. The rest moved on to another Friends' camp in North Dakota. There all Warner factions, all the differences between them dissolving into a fractious unity, settled into a single bunkhouse which they promptly named "the Casbah" and, from there, soon became one of the notorious centers of dissent and disruption in Friends' CPS.

Fifty years later, it would be gratifying to say that this imposed "corporate" Catholic witness for peace continued on into the post-war years in a permanent and more effective form. Such, alas, was not the case. A few Warnerites did involve themselves in organized peace activities and groups (the Catholic Worker, the Catholic Peace Fellowship, American PAX Society [later Pax Christi USA], etc.). Others may have maintained contact with more traditional nonsectarian peace organizations like the Fellowship of Reconciliation and the War Resisters League. The remainder, one may assume or at least hope, persisted in their private opposition to war even if they have not engaged in more organized or public expression of that opposition. But the record is not inspiring.

On the other hand, of the almost 30 Warner campers I was able to reach for my Warner study (*Another Part of the War: The Camp Simon Story*) none expressed any regrets for the stand they had taken. A few questioned whether it might not have been better to have taken a more uncompromising stand and refuse all service under conscription. Disappointing though the failure of these World War II objectors to remain active in the peace movement may be, there is some satisfaction, perhaps even pride, to be taken from one fact: if the Warner experience accomplished nothing else, it gave tangible evidence of Catholic resistance, weak and flawed though it most certainly was, to a war effort that claimed almost unanimous support. In that it represented a rejection of the dreadful excesses that marked that war and established a precedent for the more widespread Catholic opposition to war that is in evidence today. Even though we cannot claim any direct causal link between the two, the Catholic opposition to World War II prepared the ground for what was to come in the days of Vietnam.

If even this is too much to claim, the 75 men assigned to Warner can take satisfaction in knowing that, despite all its frustrations and hardships, the experience made it possible for them to at least avoid participation in the organized and planned mass destruction of human beings that found its logical culmination in the twin horrors of Auschwitz and Hiroshima. That ought to count for something. If so, the anniversary is worth noting.

11.
The Berrigans: Radical Pacifism Personified

The Catholic peace radicals of my generation are increasingly troubled by the failure of Catholic peace radicals of this generation to avoid direct or indirect association with violence. We are inclined to be suspicious of what seems to be a growing willingness to accept violence as a tactic. Today's Catholic anti-war agitators are apparently gravitating more and more in the direction of the New Left and forming alliances with groups like the Black Panthers, condoning if not actually endorsing the often senselessly disruptive and destructive acts and rhetoric such groups tend to promote.

We have, first, the introduction of direct action tactics which have gone beyond protest to actual attempts to disrupt the war effort or the operations of some agency or program related to the war effort. The series of raids upon offices of draft boards and prominent manufacturers of war materiel initiated by Rev. Philip Berrigan, S.S.J., and his fellow members of the "Baltimore Four" on October 27, 1967, and repeated by him and an expanded group, this time including his Jesuit brother Daniel (The "Catonsville Nine") on May 17, 1968, marked a dramatic new turn in radical peace action. Furthermore, as the raids proliferated throughout the country — in Milwaukee, Chicago, San Francisco, New York, Washington (here against Dow Chemical instead of the Selective Service System), Indianapolis, Minneapolis/ St. Paul, Boston — it became evident that this was an almost exclusively Catholic operation.

It would be a mistake to measure the impact of these raids only in terms of repeat performance ratios, the increasing numbers of persons involved, and the extent to which they succeeded in destroying draft files. Of at least equal importance were the "festivals" of support which drew admirers and well-wishers from all over the country as the various cases came to trial. Through these mass celebrations, and the hundreds of smaller gatherings organized to meet and talk with the "criminals" while the legal proceedings against them lumbered along, it is a conservative estimate to say that tens of thousands were reached by the action and many of these were undoubtedly moved to more direct opposition to the war.

In the face of such exciting evidence of success, it is difficult to criticize the Berrigan raids. The difficulty is greatly magnified in my own case by the fact that some of my past writings have been cited in several of the trials as factors in the decision to turn to this new level of radical peace activity. At the same time it would be less than honest to ignore the fact that strongly dissenting views have been expressed within what is usually described as the peace movement and, though I certainly do not share the more condemnatory of these judgments, I do share some of their underlying misgivings. Since these misgivings reflect the differences between the two generations of peace radicals, it is perhaps in order to discuss them briefly.

One thing must be made perfectly clear, however. In no sense are these comments to be taken as an "attack" upon the Berrigans or the others who have followed their inspiring leadership. I count them and several of their followers among my most valued personal friends, and even were this not the case, I would regard them and their commitment with awe and admiration. I have been shocked and offended by the insensitive criticisms and thoroughly unjustified condemnations directed against them by so many Catholics, including fellow priests and bishops, who seem to have a far greater capacity for indignation over the napalming of draft files than they have been able to muster over the napalming of Vietnamese civilians.

As moral witness, I would challenge the right of anyone to fault the acts of these courageous men and women, lay and religious. In the sanctuary of their individual consciences they concluded that the traditional forms of opposition to the war no longer held promise of success, that only some dramatic act of resistance and obstruction could have any impact at all upon a continuing moral evil. Once convinced of this, they decided for themselves that the prison witness has now become the only appropriate witness for the Christian who wishes to dissociate himself completely from an unjust and immoral war and the deep-seated social injustices that war is designed to perpetuate. So they acted — as, indeed, any Christian who reaches such moral convictions would be obliged to act.

This is not to say that their analysis of the situation must be accepted by everyone without question. Those of us who have not yet seen fit to join them generally do not agree that all other forms of protest and opposition have run their course. If we continue to speak and march and sign petitions, this is not to be taken as a *prima facie* confession of moral cowardice (though, in all honesty, we cannot exclude that possibility); instead it is to be read as an affirmation, possibly overly optimistic, that something can still be accomplished within and through "the system" they have rejected.

Time may well prove the Berrigans are absolutely right. It has become far more difficult to defend the potency of conventional forms of protest when we consider a President unwilling to stir from his televised football game to note the presence of a half-million American citizens marching outside to protest his policies. Add to this display of callous indifference the incredibly stupid statements periodically issued by the Vice President and other highly placed officials, and the suggestion that democratic processes have reached a final and dead end takes on new validity. When an Agnew attacks the news media, how far are we from a Goebbels? When a Julius Hoffman displays a level of judicial temperament and decorum that would have won the admiration of Roland Freisler and his *Volksgericht*, is it really enough to send off a new flurry of telegrams to Congressmen and Senators?

However one may answer these troubling questions, it is clear (or should be) that the Berrigan-style peace activism presents no problem *as personal witness* and, as such, deserves the respect and support of every committed Christian. My own problem with it is at the level of *communication*, the level at which all the differences discussed earlier become relevant to the issue. In all fairness I must add that some of the participants in these raids with whom I have discussed my misgivings object to the distinction itself, insisting that the action must be judged only as witness. Were this actually the case, however, there would have been little point in making all the elaborate arrangements to have the press — and, if possible, television cameras as well — on the scene to record the "crime."

It is clear, too, that the very symbols employed — the pouring of blood at Baltimore, the use of home-made napalm at Catonsville and in the subsequent raids — testify to an overriding intent to make a point, to get a message across as effectively as possible. This, I submit, is communication and to that extent it can be judged as communication. The first judgment to be made is that as communication it was astonishingly successful. The hundreds of supporters who rallied to the defendants' support, who traveled great distances to join the trial "celebrations" heard, understood, and accepted that message. Some of them accepted it to the point of going forth to do likewise.

If this were the whole story, the operation would have to be voted a complete success. Unfortunately, there is more to be taken into account. It is evident that tremendous numbers of people, including as already noted many already engaged in peace activities, were "turned off" by what seemed to them an altogether excessive form of protest. Certainly these included those who were already committed to support for the war effort and who were only too ready to take this as one more evidence of the unreasonableness of any dissent in wartime.

Much more serious a negative effect, however, was the amount of adverse reaction on the part of others who had been hitherto uncommitted. As a native Milwaukeean with continuing ties to that community I can testify to the strength of the opposition to the "Milwaukee Fourteen" raid, including, I might add, expressions of indignant disapproval by individuals who had provided me with support and encouragement during the full period of my service as a conscientious objector to World War II.

The only real test of the raids as communication — whether more of the uncommitted were turned off or won over — is beyond our power to determine at this time. If, as I would guess, the balance was negative, they were at least a partial failure. That some lukewarm opponents of the war were fired up to the point that they assumed a more direct and active role is an argument in the Berrigans' favor; however, this would have to be measured against others who may have been pushed or scared away.

One final point has to be made in this connection. In weighing the relative importance of the dimensions of witness and communication, the former must be given unquestioned priority. One must always act as his conscience demands, even at the price of alienating others. A hypothetical parallel might be helpful here. Had a similar group of Catholic priests and laymen invaded some offices in Nazi Germany to remove, deface, and destroy the lists of Jews scheduled for deportation to the extermination camps, few of us would be inclined to criticize them today for their "extremism." And this would hold true even if it could be shown that the majority of the "good" Germans of the time did not understand or were offended by their action. Here, too, one cannot be sure of just how "hypothetical" this parallel may be; time and added perspective may show that this is where the Berrigans and their fellow criminals are and where the rest of us should be.

One part of the Berrigan message did come through loud and clear to both the opponents and the supporters of their action. Whether so intended or not, the draft board raids contributed, on the one hand, to the new mood of radical dissent which takes it for granted that one is free to disregard and disobey any law with which he does not agree — and, on the other, to the conviction held by Mr. Nixon's "silent majority" that dissent as such is an invitation to anarchy. Both positions, it should be noted, represent a distorted understanding of a perfectly valid principle of civil disobedience, namely that an immoral or unjust law is no law and not only may be, but should be, disobeyed.

The crucial difference between this formulation and that which is in the ascendancy today is that "classic" civil disobedience is specific: the offensive law or practice, or even authority, is identified and the faults are spelled out as part of the act of disobedience itself. Increasingly this standard is being abandoned in favor of highly indiscriminate and individualized rejection of all authority which is then justified in the name of a vaguely defined and romanticized revolutionary ideal. What finally results in all too many instances is a frankly unprincipled exploitation of any or every issue or grievance in the interest of creating as much civil disruption as possible.

The resulting "polarization" is then interpreted as a value in its own right and as a means for promoting further revolutionary progress. Underlying this rationale is the highly dubious assumption that a final and forced choice between revolutionaries and reactionaries will result in the victory of the former. History would seem to argue instead that in any such ultimate confrontation, the Right, rather than right, is more likely to win out. If the much-scorned liberal is chided for his commitment to the illusion that it is still possible to use normal political processes to gain socially desirable ends, it would seem a far more dangerous illusion that a few strident slogans and random destructive outbursts will bring "the System" to a point of collapse. What these are far more likely to accomplish is to convert subtle repression into overt repression and with the approval, or at least the silent acquiescence, of the dominant majority.

One need not deny that this nation may have reached a critical point in its history where revolution, in the sense of a total and rapid restructuring of the social order, is the only way by which it can free itself for its own and the world's good from the chains of war, militarism, racism, and economic imperialism.

But if this is the situation, as I am prepared to say it is, it will require much more than the extravagant rhetoric and self-righteous posturings that pass for a revolutionary stance in some of our more activist circles. I do not, be it noted, include the Berrigans and their raids under this description. On the contrary, they could serve as models of carefully calculated and disciplined civil disobedience. I do suggest, however, that the dramatic quality of the raids, together with the sometimes excessive emotional reactions they provoked on the part of many of the young admirers who trooped to the trial celebrations, contributed to the spread of the "anything goes, anytime" mood that is so widespread among many of the younger elements of the peace — or, to be more accurate, anti-war — movement.

The latter distinction in terms is crucial, as the two massive demonstrations held on Boston Common in October 1969 and April 1970 revealed. On the surface they seemed quite similar. The October turnout of a hundred thousand people or so was almost matched by the April rally. Both represented a broad coalition of individuals and groups opposing the war in Vietnam. But here the similarity breaks down. October's was a gloriously happy affair; the crowd's enthusiasm was evidenced in the waves of applause that greeted each speaker and punctuated his or her remarks; and the speakers themselves reveled in their common purpose, playing down or avoiding altogether the ideological and tactical points of difference that separated them and their organizations.

April was something else. The tone of the gathering was sullen, even bitter, as it was exposed to a seemingly endless parade of speakers who were intensely particularistic in their various separate appeals. In place of the surges of spontaneous and enthusiastic response, individual speakers were greeted with localized applause from those segments of the crowd already in their camp while the great majority listened in silence or ignored them altogether. As for the speeches themselves, they often seemed designed to affront those listeners who were not already part of the speaker's following. Rational argumentation was replaced in many instances by reliance upon the rather limited stock of sex-related expletives and ritual clichés. Cue words ("pig") and slogans ("Right on!," "Power to the people!") were *de rigueur* for any speaker who wanted his or her full share of the scattered applause.

Perhaps the most depressing note of the whole affair was the frequency with which the representatives of one group would be openly scornful of the objectives of another. Advocates of pacifism and nonviolence were ridiculed and repudiated, one speaker using his time to call upon the thousands ostensibly gathered there to express their desire for peace to "pick up the gun." Only at the very end of the rally when the local "tribe" of *Hair* called upon the world to "let the sun shine in" did the crowd show any sign of catching fire, but by then it was too late. Most had already drifted away, bored or offended by the speakers or, in the case of a sizable segment, on their way to the night of destructive rioting and "trashing" in Harvard Square that followed.

The difference between the two events reflects a change in mood that has its expression in the substitution of the symbol of the clenched red fist for that of the dove and the olive branch. It is easy enough to understand the reason; the October rally, for all its success as an event, had been singularly unsuccessful in affecting national policy and the great outpouring of people for the November rally in Washington had been studiously ignored. The war and its casualties continued; domestic needs grew more pressing while the nation's resources were being squandered on the battlefields of Southeast Asia.

But to understand does not necessarily mean to accept the new emphasis, and this is where the old-line pacifists, the peace radicals of yesterday, have been forced to question the wisdom and the usefulness of actions and rhetoric which introduce and exploit new animosities in the interests of what appears to be an intensified commitment to violence and destruction. They find it ever more difficult to distinguish the slogans of the New Left ("We want peace, and we will use any means to get it!") from those of the ultra-hawks calling for the total destruction of those they define as enemy. The old-timers fear, and with good reason, that the tiger their young associates have chosen to ride is not heading down the paths of peace and fellowship among all men.

As the center of peace activism continues to move more and more in the direction of aggressive, even disruptive and destructive, activism, the prospects for further fragmentation within the peace movement become more certain. Directed and disciplined civil disobedience will have less appeal as the logic of events takes hold. Once again it is helpful to turn to the draft-board raids to illustrate the point. Probably the most compelling rationale for these raids was that given to one of my university classes by Tony Mullaney, a Benedictine priest, a member of the "Milwaukee Fourteen." As he explained it, every Christian has an obligation to be what he called "a public speaker" in the sense of dedicating his life and his acts to the spread of the Christian message and to work for the removal of social evil and injustice. To this end, he had "gone the route" and tried everything: he had marched and he had preached; he had signed petitions and written letters; he had picketed and participated in mass demonstrations — and all to no avail. No one, he was forced to conclude, was listening; or, if leaders heard, they did not heed. In order to make his point, to be the "public speaker" he had to be, it became necessary, he felt, to "raise the ante." For him that meant journeying to Milwaukee, invading the draft board office there, and destroying as many of its records as he could.

It is an extremely persuasive case, at least until we raise the next question: what if *that* doesn't work? And obviously it has not worked; both the war and the draft go on. Though it is possible to argue that the raised ante may have contributed to decisions to reform the draft and the proposals to abandon it altogether — and even, I suppose, to the decision to begin removing men from Vietnam — it would be difficult to establish that this was a major factor. On the other hand, there are those who would insist (with at least as much support from logic) that the draft board raids can be shown to have lost their original impact through repetition until now they can be shrugged off as little more than inconsequential nuisances.

If so, what must the next step be? Does one move on to bombing the offices themselves, first with advance warning and then, if the war still goes on, without the warning? To my knowledge these hypothetical next steps in the sequence have not been proposed by anyone involved in or sympathetic toward the Berrigan raids. Nevertheless, I would not be at all sure that there are not some peace radicals around who might be prepared to give such proposals their assent.

Which is only to say, in effect, that even the Berrigans may be in danger of slipping into my own "sometime radical" category. In fact, they may already be there. Thus, for instance, internal criticism has been voiced against the practice of waiting to be arrested after the "criminal" act is performed. As the "hit-and-run and be ready to hit-and-run again" mode of operation gains favor, it is entirely possible that the burners of draft files, like the burners of draft cards before them, may find their actions rejected as examples of ego-serving, bourgeois tokenism.

There is some evidence that the Catonsville raiders are themselves split on this issue. The decision of four of them to "go underground" as fugitives after their Supreme Court appeal was denied should not be read as an attempt to evade the personal unpleasantness of spending several years in prison. Instead, the decision represents something of an ideological shift. In Dan Berrigan's words, the purpose is to "show them they can no longer lock people up on their order, any more than they can induct people into the military service on their order." This is, of course, a perfectly acceptable rationale, and one is free to hope (as I do) that the fugitives seek to evade capture in order to continue their work against the war. This does not alter the very significant fact, however, that it is quite a different rationale from the one originally set forth.

In the early raids, the governing rationale centered upon the principles of Christian nonviolent resistance *including* the crucial spiritual dimension of accepting the penalty *because of the continued witness the penalty itself represents.* It is my recollection that some members of the Catonsville Nine, Dan Berrigan among them, were ambivalent about offering any court defense at all lest the clarity of their witness be confused and lost. Needless to say, it is not for the "guilty bystander," who would not be called upon to serve the sentence in any case, to decide which of the two formulations is the better or in which form the witness is more effective. It is the shift itself that interests me and the fact that it has been in the direction of what is generally taken to be a more radical stand.

Whether it actually is more radical or not is the final question to be raised and discussed. How one answers the question will determine who is entitled to the peace radical designation. Returning to the personal framework employed here, I have not destroyed draft records or, for that matter, draft cards (though I have violated the law by accepting draft cards turned in at a resistance rally). Nor have I encouraged others to break the law; in fact, I have argued against the draft-board raids with friends who were subsequently involved in this kind of action. If one measures radicalism by the dramatic content of an act and the degree of illegality involved, I am not (nor, I fear, have I ever been) much of a radical.

If, on the other hand, we take the term to mean a firm conviction based on an informed interpretation of fundamental moral principle and a pattern of behavior which gives expression to that conviction, all is not lost. By this standard, the conscientious objector performing his alternate service is as much a "radical" as the federal prisoner whose conscience told him that this was not enough. Of course, the CO who does recognize a moral obligation to violate the law but accepts alternate service instead could not be so designated, though his witness should not be written off completely. By the same token, the individual who is not personally convinced that it is right and necessary to violate the law but feels impelled to follow the raucous crowd which tells him that "this is where it's at," or who is swept into his activism by the appeal of greater drama and risk, should not be classified too readily as a radical either. The radicalism, in short, lies in the moral commitment, not in the manifestation alone.

If this seems a rather inconclusive note on which to end this discussion, it is nonetheless crucial. Conformism can come in many shades and forms, and a truly radical activity is more than a matter of ego-gratification through exhibitionistic extravagance. The elements of Catholic peace radicalism, as I see them, must include the following: first and most essential, a thoroughgoing commitment to the Gospel message of peace and love; second, a conviction that the Christian must always be prepared to act according to that commitment and as his conscience instructs, regardless of the consequences he may have to suffer; third, he must do so in a spirit of charity toward those not yet aware of the pacifist implications of their faith; and, finally, he must so govern his behavior that nothing he may do will violate or contradict those principles he has set out to serve.

Some may feel that such a formulation is too "open," that it includes too wide a range of individual witnesses under the rubric of radicalism. Nevertheless, to the extent that it insists upon the primacy of the individual conscience and incorporates fundamental Christian ideal of all-inclusive and self-sacrificing love, it is radical in the fullest and truest sense of the word. Which is only to suggest that the Cross, more than either the olive branch or the fist, still holds promise of being the most radical symbol of all.

This formulation I have offered allows all the room in the world for the courage and the creativity of the Berrigans and the other new-breed radicals who, quite rightly, have taken over the leadership of the Catholic peace movement; but it does so without denying or rejecting the witness of the earlier generation of peace radicals — or, for that matter, of men like Franziskus Stratmann of Germany and Paul Hanly Furfey and others in America who provided us with so great a measure of inspiration.

If, as I for one am ready and happy to acknowledge, today's radicals are more likely to succeed in finally "turning the Church around" and bringing it back to full awareness of what was its original pacifist mission, it is perhaps important that we not overlook altogether the sometime radicals who brought them to their starting point. In this sense still, if in no other, it all does go together.

12.
Thomas Merton: Nonviolence and the Spirituality of Peace

The term "prophet" is used freely these days, perhaps too freely, but we need not be hesitant about applying it to Thomas Merton. Nowhere is it more justified than in matters bearing upon Christian responsibilities with respect to war and peace. In published writings and personal communications Merton was a prophet in every sense of the term.

Like the prophets of the Old Testament he recognized the true dimensions of the corruption and evil of his time and tried to speak the saving word — sometimes in scathing denunciation of specific acts and prevailing trends; more often in inspirational exhortations calling Christians to a fuller and purer testimony to the faith they professed and a more effective performance of their personal responsibility to continue Christ's ministry of peace. If the call was ignored and those in power less responsive than the oppressors of past ages, the fault was not his. In true prophetic style he struggled on, making of his monastic cell (and later his hermitage) a center of spiritual resistance to an immoral war then in progress and, no less crucial, to the war that lies ahead, a threat to the future existence of our planet and all the creatures which inhabit it.

In this he had the prophet's gift of foresight. True, his works record no extraordinary visions or supernatural revelations. Instead, the foresight lay in his uncanny ability to see distant consequences, spiritual as well as historical, in the policies and practices of the moment. For instance, in dealing with a relatively short-lived controversy over a theologian's proposition, published in a popular Catholic journal, that a householder would be justified in shooting a less provident neighbor who tried to intrude upon the family backyard fall-out shelter, Merton saw the underlying truth that was not faced then — and one only vaguely grasped by the American bishops in their 1983 pastoral letter. He concludes his brief commentary:

> Let us for the love of heaven wake up to the fact that our own minds are just as filled with dangerous power today as the nuclear bombs themselves. And let us be very careful how we unleash the pent-up forces in the minds of others. The hour is extremely grave. The guarded statements of moral theologians are a small matter compared to the constant deluge of irresponsible opinions, criminal half-truths and murderous images disseminated by the mass media. *The problem is going to be solved in our thoughts, in our spirit, or not at all.* It is because the minds of men have become what they have become that the world is poised on the brink of total disaster. [emphasis mine]

Merton was not around — at least not in the flesh — to contribute the insights of his prophetic wisdom to the work of the Bernardin Committee charged with drafting the pastoral, yet many of his observations in published articles and his unpublished "cold war letters" find echoes in the pastoral's text. The bishops' telling image of "a new moment" which moved them to undertake a full moral analysis of nuclear war and its implications for the Church (and for all humanity) was an image familiar to this cloistered Trappist. Today what some may have dismissed in the 1960s as too apocalyptic a view of where the world was headed is at best a faint approximation of the threat we face. Jonathan Schell's book (*The Fate of the Earth*) received great attention and much praise, and deservedly so, but Merton was writing on that theme decades before. And what Schell protested as an "alliance with death" is put into even starker terms in

Merton's warning that what was really involved is nothing less than the "free choice of global suicide," a "moral evil second only to the Crucifixion."

Schell concluded his book on the hopeful note that we may yet avoid sinking into "the final coma" by awakening to the truth of our peril in time to "break through the layers of our denials, put aside our fainthearted excuses, and rise up to cleanse the earth of nuclear weapons." He does not tell us what will bring about this saving awakening, however. Merton, too, offers hope, but he expresses it in more contingent terms: "The most urgent necessity of our time is therefore not merely to prevent the destruction of the human race by nuclear war. . . . It must be possible for every free man to refuse his consent and deny his cooperation to this greatest of crimes."

There is yet another sense in which Merton deserves honor as a prophet. His influence continues and expands in the ever-escalating body of literature inspired by him and his works. And this is found not only in published articles, books, dissertations, etc. One of the sources I used in preparing this paper is the Harvard honors thesis written by a young colleague of mine at the Center on Conscience and War (John Leary) on the topic, "Contemporary Catholic Theories of Nonviolence." This young man of almost unlimited promise was deeply impressed as much by the intense spirituality of Merton's works as by their content. Dan Berrigan's tribute to this young man (". . . if Dorothy Day had had a son according to her wish, he would have been in the image of John") could apply just as well to Merton. Leary died at 24, but it is comforting to know that there are other intellectual "sons" (and "daughters" too) of Thomas Merton keeping his influence alive in this time of desperate need.

A prophet, yes — but a pacifist too? The question must be raised if only because I will be discussing the spirituality of peace from a frankly pacifist perspective and borrowing heavily from Merton to support much of what I have to say. Merton's answer — at least as it is given in several of his articles — is decidedly negative. He was concerned about the tendency of pacifism "to take on the air of a quasi-religion as though it were a kind of faith in its own right" and the inability of the pacifist "to countenance any form of war since for him to accept any war in theory or in practice would be for him to deny his faith." As he saw it, "A Christian pacifist then becomes one who compounds this ambiguity by insisting, or at least implying, that pacifism is an integral part of Christianity, with the evident conclusion that Christians who are not pacifists have, by that fact, apostatized from Christianity."

He is correct in everything he says — up to that howler of a non sequitur at the end. It would take a gross display of spiritual elitism and pride (to which, I confess, *some* pacifists are prone) to ignore the fact that pacifism is still not accepted by the majority of today's Christians or to attribute that disagreeable fact to pandemic apostasy. Most pacifists I know (and this certainly is true in my case) do not fall into that tempting trap. They are more likely to follow the example of Franz Jaegerstaetter, the martyred Austrian peasant so admired by Merton, who when asked to explain why he stood alone in his refusal to serve in Hitler's army replied that his fellow Christians, including his bishop, had not been "given the grace" to see the immorality such service would represent.

Perhaps even such a claim to a special grace of insight might strike one as too condescending. All the pacifist says of those who do not see things his way and accept orders to go to war is that they are wrong (though not necessarily culpably wrong); or, if they do recognize and ignore the departure from Christian truth in the orders to kill and destroy and still persist in their obedience, they are the unfortunate victims of weakness of will. This still sounds judgmental, and probably is, but it makes allowance, with regret, for the person who in perfectly good (however erroneous) conscience accepts war and service in war.

Again, was Merton pacifist? My answer is that, based on his writings and their analysis of how we came to be what we are and what it will take to change, he was more of a pacifist than he was ready to admit — perhaps more than he was aware. There are points at which his and my positions differ, but they are few and not of major consequence. In its essentials my view of the spirituality of peace and its expression in protest and prayer finds support and validation in Merton's work. In some respects, it finds its origin there as well.

It is because of this support and validation that I presume to address the subject not only from the pacifist perspective but from that of professional sociologist as well. This may seem to be a kind of scholarly heresy since sociology, as many practitioners of the discipline would insist, can have little to offer in so non-empirical a realm as the innermost structures of an individual's religious commitment. Merton, of course, would have his own objections, having once gone so far as to thank God that he was not a sociologist!

He was wrong there too. Whatever else "spirituality" may mean and however much it is formed and sustained by the indefinable and immeasurable quality of divine grace, as a motive force in the individual's behavior it takes effect and operates through that individual's perceptions. The content and behavioral implications of such perceptions make it a proper subject of study in the sociology of religion.

To treat spirituality as a complex of motivating perceptions is not to reduce it to the level of the mundane. On the contrary, it contributes to a deeper understanding of the ways in which internalized values find expression in external acts and behavior. Does this mean that since every individual's perceptions must be his, or hers, alone that each person's "spirituality" becomes *ad hoc* and, in a sense, *sui generis*? Yes — and no. This would be true were it not for the processes of socialization which, even as they mold each of us into the unique persons we become, provide us with patterned similarities as well. From infancy on our development is guided, sometimes determined, through exposure to the same institutions (especially family, school, and church) and less structured, though still culturally conditioned, life experiences. Each individual and each individual's spirituality are "unique," but that uniqueness is better understood in most cases as a variation on a theme.

The principal components of the spirituality of peace are the perception one has of God; the perception of the proper relationship between believer and God (extending to the proper relationship of believer to believer); and the perception of the ultimate purpose and goal of those relationships. I would go so far as to suggest that any conceptualization of spirituality would have to begin with these.

Nor is there anything particularly unique in the basic perception the pacifist has of God as all-powerful, all-knowing and, most important of all, infinitely loving and forgiving. His is the power to judge and to punish those who reject Him and His way to choose the path of evil, just as He promises eternal rewards to those who fulfill His will.

Pretty standard stuff to this point, one would agree. Nor do pacifists differ from their fellow Christians in the belief that this God became incarnate in the One whose followers we profess to be as a means of redeeming and saving His human creations. Unlike Homer's jealous divinities on Mt. Olympus toying with their human pawns as it might suit their passing moods or fancy, the God of the Christian has more respect and infinitely more exalted plans for us. As Merton put it, this God "has chosen for Himself, in the Mystical Body of Christ, an elect people, regenerated by the Blood of the Savior and committed by their baptismal promise to wage war with the great enemy of peace and salvation."

At this point, though, we do encounter a crucial point. The God of the *pacifist* Christian, because He has such respect and plans, would never seek to prove a point or display even righteous anger by condemning millions of innocent men, women and children to the dread scourge of war — and it certainly would not be His intent that those who claim to be His followers become the instruments of destruction and mass slaughter. Instead (Merton again), "He brought to His disciples a vocation and a task, to struggle in the world of violence to establish His peace not only in their own hearts but in society itself." That wars come about through human fault and weakness cannot be denied, nor can we ignore the suffering and oppression they bring. But to attribute them to the punitive excesses of an angered Lord of Righteousness is to miss the point completely. The Christian is called to confront these evils in a spirit of sincere remorse, coupled with a firm attitude of complete confidence in — indeed, *abandonment to* — the saving goodness of God's will. In this we have moved to the consideration of that second basic perception, the relationship between God and believer. This is not to be mistaken for a fatalistic resignation to "what will be" but, instead, an active acceptance of that vocation of peace and whatever it may require. Merton's "Prayer of Abandonment" expresses this beautifully:

> My Lord God
> I have no idea where I am going.
> I cannot see the road ahead of me
> and I do not know for certain where it will end.
> Nor do I know myself,
> and the fact that I think I am following your will
> does not mean that I am actually doing so.
> But I believe
> that the desire to please you
> does in fact please you.
> And I hope
> that I have that desire in all that I am doing.
> I hope I will never do anything apart from that desire.
> And I know that if I do this
> you will lead me by the right road,
> though I may know nothing about it.
> Therefore will I trust you always.
> Though I may seem to be lost and in the shadow of death,
> I will not fear,
> for you are ever with me,
> and will never leave me
> to face my perils alone.

Since we are all members of the same Mystical Body, this special quality of the relationship with God should carry over to our relationship with one another as well. "If we are disciples of Christ," Merton writes, "we are necessarily our brother's keeper. . . . We cannot give an irresponsible and unchristian consent to the demonic use of power for the destruction of a whole nation, a whole continent, or possibly even the whole human race."

No better statement of the spirituality of peace as it bears upon our relationships with others can be found than the familiar peace prayer of St. Francis. One pleads to be made an instrument of peace, to learn to replace hatred with love, injury with pardon, despair with hope — and so on. That term "instrument" must be understood properly, however. It does not imply a self-abnegating depersonalization making one a "tool" in the mechanistic sense; rather, it calls for a fully reasoned and freely willed surrender of self in total commitment — in that spirit of total, yet confident, abandonment so movingly expressed in Merton's prayer.

This is the "other side" of the pacifist's perception of God, and from it we derive the pacifist alternative to war and preparation for war, the theory and practice of nonviolence. We are told, and as Christians we presumably accept, that God's power is made perfect and manifest in our human infirmity; that no matter how perilous our situation may be, the gates of hell will not prevail. Of course this is no guarantee of "victory" or "success" as the world may define them; history provides evidence enough that those who appear to be the "good guys" are all too often victimized by the bad. But the same uncertainty of outcome is present in war — with the crucial difference that in war there is the certainty that people, all too often innocent people, will be hurt and killed. Now, given the nature of modern weaponry and the stated intent of national leaders to use it, the future existence of the planet is placed in doubt. One often hears the false charge that pacifists are indifferent to evil and the need to combat it. The commitment to nonviolence as an alternative to war is not indifference but, rather, a refusal to succumb to the delusion that it is somehow possible to overcome evil by adding to it.

Merton is too widely recognized as one of the leading apostles of Christian nonviolence to need citation on this point. His writings on the subject are so extensive and compelling that I do not hesitate to repeat what I have said elsewhere, that this will prove to be his major and most enduring contribution. As such they stand alone in their own right, but they also provide the transition to the third of the basic components mentioned earlier, the pacifist's perception of the ultimate purpose and goal to which we as Christians are committed. In his "Footnote to Ulysses" he distinguished between nonviolence as the pursuit of truth (the nonviolence of the strong which can never fail) and nonviolence as a means to power (the nonviolence of the weak which carries no similar promise of success). It is surprising to find this admirer of Martin Luther King and ardent supporter of the civil rights movement (even, at times, its more radical Black Power variant!) striking a note which seems to distance himself from both. He writes of nonviolence: "It does not say 'We shall overcome' so much as 'This is the day of the Lord, and whatever may happen to us, *He* shall overcome.' " It is here in the eschatological dimension of nonviolent resistance that Merton makes his most significant contribution to the spirituality of peace.

His frequent use of the term, "post-Christian era," takes on a double meaning in the context of nonviolence. Most obvious, of course, is the lesson that Christians can no longer act (assuming they ever could!) in the confidence that secular authorities will take Christian principles into account in formulating their programs and policies, especially those related to international relations and conflict. The long history of warfare does not provide many — one might suggest *any* — instances of ruler or generals incorporating the limits imposed by the conditions of the "just war" so carefully elaborated by St. Thomas and others into their strategic planning or military operations. However fervently the rhetoric of war might continue to extol religious themes and virtues, one cannot ignore the fact that the missiles launched from even a "blessed" Trident submarine (the "Auschwitz of Puget Sound," as Archbishop Hunthausen named it) were designed and are intended to commit precisely those "offenses against God and man himself" condemned by Vatican II.

It is as Merton said: "We are no longer living in a Christian world. . . . Today a non-Christian world still retains a few vestiges of Christian morality, a few formulas and cliches, which serve on appropriate occasions to adorn indignant editorials and speeches. But otherwise we witness deliberate campaigns to oppose and eliminate all education in Christian truth and morality."

There is another, more profound, sense in which ours is a "post-Christian era," however. This *is* the Day of the Lord. Christ *has* come. The Kingdom *is* here, within us. Not in the fullness of its promised glory, perhaps, but the promise is still there for all who accept it and live their lives accordingly. In terms of the spirituality of peace, whatever sufferings we may have to face are as nothing compared with the moral danger that lies in the temptation to repay violence with violence and, by so doing, turn away from Him and the protection He will provide. Taken in this perspective, the insane rush for security through new weapons of ever-increasing destructiveness is a betrayal of the true security which is the Christian's for the asking.

Again, in Merton's words, "It is no exaggeration to say that our times are apocalyptic in the sense that we seem to have come to a point at which all the hidden, mysterious dynamism of the 'history of salvation' revealed in the Bible has flowered into final and decisive crisis. The term 'end of the world' may or may not be one that we are capable of understanding. But at any rate we seem to be assisting at the unwrapping of the mysteriously vivid symbols of the last book of the New Testament. In their nakedness, they reveal to us our own selves as the men whose lot it is to live in the time of a possibly ultimate decision. In a word, the end of the world is quite really and quite literally up to us and to our immediate descendants, if any. And this, I might venture to suggest, is more 'apocalyptic' than anything our fathers discovered in the Revelations of St. John."

The three major themes, or components, of the spirituality of peace — at least as I have presented them — seem to leave little room for Merton's (or the bishops') persistence in defending the *theory* of justifiable war. There is evidence enough in his writings that he was aware that in *practice* the traditional formulations are almost totally irrelevant to the reality of modern war and nuclear war in particular. It is tempting to speculate on where he would be today, now that bishops have re-discovered and legitimized (though not yet endorsed) the kind of pacifism he so regularly rejected. Pointless, too — for whether he accepted the label or not, his books and articles are there to provide support for those who do.

They also provide invaluable guidelines to how the spirituality of peace can be given expression in the behavior of individuals. There is an unfortunate tendency on the part of many, including pacifists, to speak in terms of a dichotomy: a choice between prayer and similar forms of spiritual activity on the one hand and involvement in direct action protests on the other.

I prefer to see the two options as the opposite ends of a single continuum with the actual positions taken located in between, each representing the "mix" of both best suited to the individual's unique variation on the spirituality theme (a) as determined by the circumstances of his or her life. Thus one might expect a strictly cloistered contemplative (or the kind of isolated hermit that Merton yearned to be but never was) would have precious little opportunity or inclination to engage in outward protest, relying instead on prayer and other devotional or penitential practices to halt the drift toward the war that is forbidden.

Parents, too, might find familial responsibilities too demanding to permit the "luxury" of risking arrest or prison for civil disobedience or other forms of activism. Some might even have difficulty finding the time to engage in legal demonstrations.

In neither case need protest activity be eliminated altogether. There are always letters to be written, petitions to be distributed and signed, vigils and picketing and the like to be done. Heads of households have gone further to engage in symbolic tax resistance, although few are in a position to risk their family's welfare by refusing to pay taxes altogether or renouncing taxable earnings. For their part, religious communities, in addition to participating in some kind of tax resistance, might give thought to the possibility of making themselves havens of sanctuary for "criminals of conscience" — taking as their model their counterparts in Europe which provided sanctuary for Jews and saved many from Nazi extermination camps.

Even those monasteries and convents which will concentrate on prayer and penance as their most proper expression of the spirituality of peace can reach out to the consciences of others through teaching and works of scholarship. Merton himself is the best example of what can be done in this respect. Despite the confines of Trappist life — and even though silenced for a time by superiors who considered it "unseemly" for a monk to involve himself in public controversy — he found it possible to bring "respectability" to a position which, until then, had been dismissed by many of his fellow Catholics as bordering on heresy. Nor was this all. He was indirectly responsible for more direct action protest on the part of others not subject to those limitations. His 1964 retreat on "The Spiritual Roots of Protest" was especially significant. Within a short time most of his retreatants were in prison for various actions of public protest. One might go so far as to suggest that the "Great Catholic Peace Conspiracy" of the Vietnam years had its real beginning in the quiet setting of Gethsemani.

If it is difficult to conceive of prayer by itself as an effective or sufficient peace witness, this is even more true of the other pole of the continuum. No matter how "extreme" or "disruptive," direct action protest can draw inspiration and support from prayer. The Berrigans and their followers offer striking evidence of how this works. In the eyes of the law, this loose and widespread network of separate but "affinity-minded" groups constitutes a criminal "underground." Nevertheless, all their actions — whether blocking entry to nuclear facilities, climbing fences to destroy weapons components, digging graves on the White House lawn, or pouring blood on the Pentagon — can be seen as spiritual events and experiences. They begin with sessions of common prayer and reflection in which participants make themselves open to a "call" to specific acts of civil disobedience. Once the decision is made, there is more prayer and meditation to help find the strength and confidence needed to face up to the chosen task and the penalties it could bring. Finally, after the deed is done — the blood poured, the ashes strewn, the missile cones damaged — the "criminals" join in prayer again while they await arrest.

Not all direct action is confrontational; indeed, Merton, among others, voiced concern against the danger of escalation beyond peaceful protest — "in which case," as he put it, "it may also be escalating into self-contradiction." It is, again, a question of determining the right "mix" for each, which in turn depends upon that uniqueness of the individual's spirituality within the limits set by the components I have identified.

Merton was concerned that the Berrigan-type actions represented a kind of desperation that might frighten rather than edify the uncommitted public. He had a profound respect for someone like Dorothy Day, who, though ever willing to refuse cooperation she felt contributed to war or the war mentality and ready to go to jail for her belief in peace, did so without seeking publicity. And he had the highest praise for a Franz Jaegerstaetter who was not "confrontational" at all but still accepted martyrdom rather than submit to the state's demand that he take part in an unjust war. It is well to note, though, he waited until he actually received induction orders to make his heroic refusal.

Anyone familiar with the lives of Dorothy Day and Franz Jaegerstaetter knows how much prayer and penance meant to them and the part these played in providing and sustaining the commitment behind Dorothy's lifelong practice of the spiritual and corporal works of mercy and Jaegerstaetter's refusal to violate his conscience. Too often, though, we write them off as exceptional cases (which, of course, they are) beyond normal spiritual capacities (which they are not).

In the final analysis, the spirituality of peace is more than the perceptions from which it draws content and form, and to this extent it goes beyond the reach of sociology. The perceptions can be objectified and classified, even analyzed in terms of psychological and cultural implications. But it is the quality of commitment that counts, and this involves something extra that escapes even most imaginative methods and techniques social science can devise. That "something extra" is the touch of grace of which Jaegerstaetter spoke, the grace which informs the intellect and strengthens the will. As Christians we believe that grace will be made available to us — if we but accept it.

More than a half-century ago, the eminent sociologist, Pitirim Sorokin, traced what he called "the crisis of our age" to a shift from a culture keyed to the higher realms of spirit and mind to one in which perceptions and behavior were increasingly dominated by material and sensual concerns and values. If his analysis still holds true — and I, for one, believe it does — the crisis will not be resolved unless and until the direction of this shift is reversed.

A first and necessary step would be for each of us, man or woman, to make a personal reassessment of his or her spiritual commitments and the answers we give to those three basic questions: what do I believe about God? how do I relate to God and to my fellow human beings? do I have faith and confidence enough to take risks he may ask of me as an individual (and of us as a people) to turn away from policies and preparations which would destroy the world and humanity to "save" them?

The answer we give will determine whether that gift of grace will be recognized as such and accepted. Merton had his answer and considered it important enough to repeat in several of his essays on the subject of peace and nuclear war.

Let it serve as my conclusion:

> It is no longer reasonable or right to leave all decisions to a largely anonymous power elite that is driving us all, in our passivity, towards ruin. We have to make ourselves hear.
>
> Every individual Christian has a grave responsibility to protest clearly and forcibly against trends that lead inevitably to crimes which the Church deplores and condemns. Ambiguity, hesitation, and compromise are no longer permissible. We must find some new and constructive way of settling international disputes. This may be extraordinarily difficult. Obviously war cannot be abolished by mere wishing. Severe sacrifices may be demanded and the results will hardly be visible in our day. We still have time to do something about it, but the time is rapidly running out.

13.
Franz Jaegerstaetter: Martyr for Conscience

It is perhaps best to begin at the end — or, at least, what seemed at the time to be the end. On August 9, 1943, a thirty-seven-year-old farmer was beheaded in Berlin for refusing to serve in the German army. Shortly before, he had been visited by his wife and a priest from the tiny village in Austria where he had lived his entire life. They had come to make a final effort to change his mind and save his life, but as always they failed. Not even the thought of the three little daughters left at home could weaken his resolve — though it was clear that knowing he would never see them again caused him great emotional strain. He had long since learned to bear such strain, however. From the time he made his decision, through the months spent in prison in Linz and Berlin, he had known what the penalty would be and was prepared to accept it.

The man's name was Franz Jaegerstaetter. The village from which his journey to the executioner's block was St. Radegund, a cluster of buildings on the boundary between Germany and what had been Austria until 1938 when, following a "protective" invasion by Nazi forces, the Austrians voted almost unanimously to become a part of Hitler's Third Reich.

Franz was the only man in St. Radegund to vote against legitimizing the *fait accompli*. Such opposition was nothing new for him. Even before Hitler gained power in Germany, this simple peasant saw the evil in the Nazi movement and its program. Not only did he recognize in Hitler a threat to his beloved Austria; in his eyes, he was a dangerous and dedicated enemy of the Church Jaegerstaetter loved even more.

Through the years of Nazi domination, he was never hesitant about voicing his opposition. He apparently had no contact with the Austrian underground. Nor was he aware of its activity in the surrounding area. His opposition was personal and expressed at every opportunity in arguments with friends and fellow villagers. Most of them, he knew, caught up as they were in the enthusiasm for the *Fuehrer* and the promised "Thousand-year Reich," did not welcome being told they were wrong. In time the arguments became so predictable and often so heated that he stopped dropping in at the local *Gasthaus* for the customary stein of beer or glass of wine after a hard day's work in the fields. When greeted with the Nazi salute, *"Heil Hitler!"* he responded with the traditional *Gruss Gott* delivered with emphasis. Sometimes he substituted a scornful *Pfui Hitler* instead.

He made every effort to separate himself and his family from the detested "New Order," even refusing to accept government benefits like the family allowance to which he was entitled and emergency assistance provided after his crops were destroyed in a severe hail storm. He advised his young godson who helped on the farm against becoming a member of the Hitler Youth because of its anti-religious doctrine and activities.

Surprisingly enough, he never had serious problems with the local authorities. One assumes, then, that he did meet production quotas — but, even here, he may have tried to limit his contribution to the regime and its war effort. A decision to sell a piece of his farm brought criticism from his mother (and his response that his "few kernels" would not save Hitler). Neighbors remember, too, that he would pack his knapsack with farm produce and meat to take to some of the poorer people in the vicinity. This was seen as an act of charity — which it undoubtedly was, especially considering that his own family was not too well off; but it could also have been a way of evading Nazi regulations and keeping some of the fruits of his labor out of the wartime economy. A kind of hidden sabotage in a sense.

The failure of Nazi authorities to remove this stubborn and outspoken peasant from the scene before he left them no alternative with his outright refusal to serve can be traced to the tightness of the social network found in such small and isolated villages. The inhabitants "take care of their own," even one who insisted upon making himself obnoxious. For their part the Gestapo may have decided it was the better part of wisdom to ignore the "troublemaker" lest moving to punish him might create a worse problem by antagonizing a community that obviously was paying no attention to him and his opinions.

The village pastor was less fortunate. Like Franz a dedicated opponent of the Nazis, he and his troublesome parishioner had spent many evenings sharing their disapproval of the state of affairs in the world and in the village. He had argued against Franz's lack of prudence in voting against *Anschluss* (on the grounds that it was a pointless risk and would only serve to identify him as a suspicious malcontent); when the time came, he would be just as strong in his efforts to convince Franz not to refuse military service. For some critical comments in one of his sermons Fr. Karobath was reported to the Gestapo, briefly imprisoned, and then placed under *Bezirksverbot*, a limited exile from his parish and surrounding area and was not on the scene when the induction orders arrived. An interesting illustration of that "taking care of one's own" principle: the man suspected of making the report was ostracized by his fellow villagers — with one exception. Franz believed in the man's innocence and spoke out in his defense and was later proven right.

So what led him to take the path to heroic disobedience and martyrdom? There was nothing in his early life to indicate he would become an "enemy of the state" and a martyr to his faith in the process. Born in 1907, the illegitimate son of a young man in a nearby village who was killed in World War I, he was adopted by Heinrich Jaegerstaetter, the "Leherbauer" (in rural Austria families are identified by the traditional name of the land they occupy and farm), in 1917 after his marriage to Franz's mother. Since that marriage proved childless, Franz succeeded his step-father as "Leherbauer" after the latter's death in 1933. As a child he appears to have done well enough in the village one-room *Volkschule* though friends told of his giving the religion instructor some harried moments by pressing questions about Scripture beyond the good priest's competence to answer. Whether this was an early sign of intellectual independence in matters religious or nothing more than the bright boys' familiar game of making things difficult for teacher is impossible to say. If there was any sign of the man who in later years would keep a written and remarkably incisive record of religious meditations and devotional behavior, it escaped everyone's notice. In adolescence and young manhood he is remembered as a dutiful son and hard worker but, even more, as a popular and fairly wild rascal. He liked to drink, play cards, dance, chase after girls — and fight. The image one gets is that of a bold and irrepressible leader of an unruly band of his peers. He earned a few days in jail for leading his "gang" into a pitched battle with members of a private paramilitary force which was policing the border area surrounding St. Radegund. This was not a protest foreshadowing his rejection of military service, however; with Franz as leader, the young men of St. Radegund were "protecting their turf" against uniformed outsiders who were offering serious competition with the local girls.

The most vivid memory people have of the Franz of early days is that he introduced the first motorcycle to the community. This was mentioned so frequently in interviews that it is difficult to decide which holds priority in the villagers' minds today — the wild young man racing about the countryside on his motorcycle or the devout sacristan whose religious fanaticism brought him to a tragic end. It was the former, though, who clearly ranked higher in their affections.

Everyone spoke of "the big change," but , here too, it is difficult to trace what brought it about. For a time, it seems, some difficulty between him and another young man of the village caused enough internal dissension to threaten the peace of the community with the result that both of them were "exiled" for a time. Some versions tell of an argument over disputed property boundaries, but most claim not to know or to have forgotten the reason for the clash. Another possibility is that Franz, having fathered an illegitimate child, violated local mores by "letting the girl sit." Perhaps it could have been a case of disputed paternity (though Franz apparently acknowledged the child was his). Both hypotheses fall short, however, since the child was born in 1934, apparently some time after he had returned from "exile." The most likely explanation, some feel, is that he just left for a time to work in the mines and earn some money — out of which, it seems, he purchased the famous motorcycle.

Although fathering the child episode suggests that he picked up where he had left off, it soon became evident that he was a different man in one important respect. He had always observed the standards of religious practice normal for young men of his age and state of life; now there was a dramatic difference. One may question whether the change was as sudden or as drastic as the villagers remember, but the jolly and headstrong young ruffian became a zealous and introspective believer. He began to attend church and receive the Sacrament daily, a practice ordinarily reserved for elderly women in the rural culture. Other devotional actions began to stir comment (for the most part critical since it was assumed they competed with and detracted from his farm responsibilities). He was known to sing hymns while at work in the fields and even stop what he was doing to read the Bible or jot down pious observations or reflections that occurred to him. One story, almost certainly an exaggeration, had him praying to the flowers!

In 1937 he married and, to the surprise of the villagers and possibly the bride, took her to Rome for their honeymoon. While there they visited the usual religious shrines and attended one of the public audiences of the reigning Pontiff, Pius XI. It was only natural that the impression would spread (it is still strong) that marriage to a pious and deeply committed woman caused the "big change" — and it was not regarded by all, probably not by most, as a change for the better. The popular and rambunctious (*lustig* was the term most regularly encountered) young rowdy was replaced by a zealot whose religious fanaticism, many still believe, unhinged his mind and doomed him to a tragic and untimely death. The judgment took on more accusatory overtones in the mind of those who blamed his wife for encouraging his devotional excesses and, by implication, sharing responsibility for what was to happen.

They were wrong, of course. Franz was not "led astray" by an overly devout wife, though it is very likely that her piety had attracted him to her in the first place. Pastor Karobath told me that, shortly after Franz's return to the village — apparently before his step-father's death and certainly before he met his future bride — he had expressed an intention to join a religious order. The priest talked him out of the idea, reminding him that as heir he had the obligation to take over the operation of the Leherbauer land.

Nor is the assumption that Mrs. Jaegerstaetter encouraged her husband in his refusal of military service correct. She insists that, though she certainly did not want him to die, she left the decision to him as a matter to be decided in his personal conscience. There is some indication that she may have put more pressure on him to reconsider than she admits or, perhaps, may have realized at the time. In his prison letters Franz always took pains to stress his obligation to follow the path he had chosen. In several letters, too, he advises her to postpone a visit to the Linz prison until something definite has been decided about his case — more of a desire, perhaps, to avoid a "temptation" he was not sure he could resist?

His transfer to Berlin came suddenly and without advance warning. If he had been avoiding the strain of a face-to-face meeting, that now seemed safely out of the question. Not really, though. After the trial and the sentence to death, his court-appointed "defender" advised the priest who had replaced Fr. Karobath that if he and Mrs. Jaegerstaetter came to Berlin and convinced her husband to withdraw his refusal, there was still a chance he might be saved. The visit took place, but the condemned man would not change his mind. Though she and the priest made their pleas she was resigned to leaving the final decision to him.

Before his refusal and request he had written a set of commentaries on the situation facing Catholics in Hitler's Third Reich. In the first of these he described a dream he had several years before, about the time National Socialism was "breaking in (or, better, creeping in) upon us with all of its many different organizations." In that dream he saw a splendid, shining train circling a mountain. Everyone, including little children, were rushing to board that train. Suddenly he heard a voice warning, "This train is going to Hell." At least three years had passed, but the memory of that train remained vivid in his mind — so vivid he had come to accept it as a kind of revelation. As he interpreted it, the train represented Nazism and the eager throngs were those, Catholics included, who scrambled to join its ranks. For Franz the message was clear: that "train" was indeed headed for Hell and he, for one, was not going to ride along.

But all was not lost. "It is still possible for us, even today, to lift ourselves with God's help out the mire in which we are stuck and win eternal happiness — if only it we make a sincere effort and bring all our strength to the task." The strength was there just for the taking. Christ had come and through His death canceled the debt of sin. There was no need for Him to be crucified again to bring Christians to the awareness of what was asked of them. In another commentary ("Is There Still a God?") he took comfort and strength in spiritual optimism: "It may well be that hell holds great power over the world at the present time, but even this need not cause us Christians to fear. May the power of hell be ever so great, God's power is still greater."

It was in this spirit that he refused to take any part in what he knew was an unjust war being waged by that hell-bent regime. Today there are still those in St. Radegund who are ready to criticize, even condemn, him for the stubborn refusal to listen to the more sensible advice of others (including all the priests to whom he turned and his bishop as well). Others, more charitable perhaps, see that unwillingness as further tragic evidence that religious extremism had caused him to lose his mental bearings.

The severest critics charge him with failing in his responsibilities as a father and that he was lacking in love for his wife and children. That this is the cruelest irony of all is evident in the heart-rending letters he wrote from prison, each with a special little message for the three little girls. Most touching were the concluding lines of what appears to have been a draft of his farewell letter from his Berlin cell: "Now, my dear children, when Mother reads this letter to you, your father will already be dead. He would have loved to come to you again, but the Heavenly Father willed it otherwise. Be good and obedient children and pray for me so that we may soon be reunited in heaven."

It is best not to censure the villagers too harshly, however, for their inability to understand or approve of what he did. In purely human terms his sacrifice does make little sense. The chaplain who accompanied Franz to his execution understood. He visited the condemned man and offered to read and pray with him in preparation. His offer was quietly, but politely, declined with the explanation, "I am completely bound in inner union with the Lord and any reading would only interrupt my communication with my God." Not only would those words stay in the priest's memory, but the man's eyes shone with such joy and confidence that he could never lose the memory of that glance. Later, describing the calm and composed manner in which Franz walked to the guillotine, he told a group of Austrian nuns working in the hospital where he was in residence, "I can only congratulate you on this countryman of yours who lived as a saint and has now died a hero. I say with certainty that this simple man is the only saint I have ever met in my lifetime."

A short distance north of St. Radegund is its *Kreisstadt*, Braunau-am-Inn, the birthplace of Adolf Hitler. Somewhat farther on lies Linz, the provincial capital and the childhood home of Eichmann. It is a remarkable coincidence (or something more perhaps?) which finds these three men native to the same Upper Austrian locality: one, the dictator who terrorized the civilized world and was responsible for the slaughter of millions of human beings in extermination camps and wars; one, his willing servant and collaborator in the infamy of the Final Solution; the third, a simple peasant armed with nothing more than the vision of a shining train and an unshakeable faith in the weapons of the Spirit who chose death rather than play what he called "the crooked game."

They are all dead now, but it is the peasant whose witness lives on as a source of inspiration to others who find themselves facing situations with even greater potential for evil — including the possible annihilation of the world itself. There are no memorials to Hitler or Eichmann, but the tiny church in St. Radegund has become a place of pilgrimage.

Part II

After starting with what seemed at the time to be the end, we finish with what promises to be a beginning. A commission appointed by the current Bishop of Linz has recently completed its investigation preliminary to recommending the canonization of Franz Jaegerstaetter and submitting his cause to Rome. This is only the latest in a growing list of actions honoring his memory. Kurt Waldheim's predecessor as President of Austria issued a special award of honor citing him for having contributed to the liberation of the nation. In 1987 Bishop Aichern marked what would have been Franz's eightieth birthday by a three-day commemoration that ended with solemn Vespers in the Linz Cathedral concelebrated with Bishop Thomas Gumbleton, the Bishop President of Pax Christi USA. For twenty years or more there has been an annual candlelight walk drawing people from great distances to the martyr's grave in the St. Radegund churchyard on the anniversary of his execution. Commemorative ceremonies are celebrated in a number of countries, including Great Britain and the United States. The famous *Votivekirche* on Vienna's Ring has a full-length window portraying his defiance. There are undoubtedly other memorials of which I am not aware.

From Franz's perspective, of course, such recognition is welcome but really not all that important. There was, after all, nothing to be added. As he would insist, his witness was complete with the descent of the executioner's blade. We have Mrs. Jaegerstaetter's assurance that he never expected anyone outside of his family (and those directly involved in his trial and execution) would know or care. What he did was, and always had been, a matter between him and his God.

If his last days were burdened with the concern for his family and the thought they might suffer reprisal as relatives of a convicted enemy of the Nazi state, there was another, possibly more troubling, fear that haunted him. To have rejected the unanimous advice he had received from priests and his bishop — not to mention his court-appointed attorney's assurances of a reprieve were he to withdraw his refusal — could be viewed by some (indeed, had been suggested by some) as a kind of suicide. Was the death he had foreseen from the very start a temptation to that most serious sin?

He did not put that fear into words, but he comes close in that early draft of what he intended to be his farewell message to friends and family: "Moreover, though people charge me with a crime and have condemned me to death as a criminal, I take comfort in the knowledge that not everything which this world considers a crime is a crime in the eyes of God. And I hope that I need not fear the eternal Judge because of this crime."

As things turned out, his expectation that his death would go unnoticed came close to being fulfilled. Following the execution his body was cremated, and the prison chaplain preserved the ashes for burial in a private Berlin cemetery. At war's end they were taken to St. Radegund and given a ceremonial re-burial next to the wall of the church he had served as sacristan. There was a local controversy when Pastor Karobath, now returned to his parish, insisted on including Franz's name on the parish memorial honoring men from the village who perished in the two world wars. The returned veterans objected strongly, but Karobath had the advantage since the memorial was erected on the church's property.

A Solomonic compromise was struck by listing Franz's name at the end preceded by the phrase *Seinem Gewissen folgend* (Following his conscience). Then one of the women of the parish protested that her husband, "missing in action" on the Russian front, had been omitted from the list. To make room for the last minute addition, the phrase was struck and Jaegerstaetter's name, though out of alphabetical order, is otherwise indistinguishable from the rest.

Other than that, there was nothing. No recognition from the Linz diocese, not even a notice in the diocesan press. One article praising him as a martyr almost reached publication but was rejected at the personal intervention of the bishop he had visited before his arrest. The bishop's explanation to the editor was that while one could honor the man for being true to his conscience, he was not to be treated as a model for others to follow. In the bishop's mind, the true heroes were those who had fought and died. It is greatly to Bishop Aichern's credit that this wrong has been righted.

It was not until almost twenty years after the execution that a series of providential accidents made me privileged to "discover" Jaegerstaetter. After a summer spent in "on the scene" research, interviewing his wife and daughters and the friends and neighbors who had known him, my book (*In Solitary Witness: The Life and Death of Franz Jaegerstaetter*) was published. A German edition, published three years later, was enthusiastically received and served as the basis for a major television production by ORF, the Austrian national network. Scheduled for prime-time showing on the major national holiday, it drew so much favorable attention that it was repeated a few weeks later, this time in conjunction with 500 scheduled discussion groups addressing the topic, "Did he do the right thing?" The program was later distributed as a film and won major prizes at an international religious film festival.[1]

During the debate on the Vatican Council's *Pastoral Constitution on the Church in the Modern World*, an English archbishop, Thomas D. Roberts, S.J., submitted an intervention on conscientious objection recommending Jaegerstaetter as a source of inspiration and guidance to the assembled bishops of the entire world. That would have pleased the man who worried that he might have been committing a sin by not following his bishop's advice.

In the United States the peasant's example was widely cited in the many debates and protests against the war in Vietnam. At a Boston ceremony at which young men turned in their draft cards as an act of civil disobedience, I was stunned to hear a voice come over the loudspeaker saying, "I am a seminarian. . . . I am here because of an Austrian peasant named Franz Jaegerstaetter." The seminarian became a priest, joined the Fathers Berrigan in the Milwaukee Fourteen "draft-board raid," and ended up in prison. A moving story, but carrying more impact on national policy was Daniel Ellsberg's admission that reading the story of Jaegerstaetter's heroic sacrifice for conscience was one of the influences that led him to release the Pentagon Papers, a decision that hastened the end of the Vietnam war. That simple peasant of whom no one was ever supposed to hear, helped change *our* history a generation later and an ocean away!

There is an important lesson to be learned from this: *no witness is lost.* This is not to deny that there must have been others who perished alone and whose stories have been lost to history as history is recorded by fallible human beings.

Even so, the principle holds true for all of them. In the divine economy it is the act and the intent that counts. Jaegerstaetter knew

---

[1]Because it was based on my book, Pax Christi USA was given permission to arrange showings of the film (on a non-commercial basis) in the United States and, later, to have videotape copies made for rental or sale. For information about the film and its availability, write the author c/o Pax Christi USA, 348 E. Tenth St., Erie, PA 16503.

this and was ready and willing to embrace the anonymity he was certain would be his lot. (In this connection, one unanticipated benefit from my "discovery" is that at least three others have since been brought to attention and given the honor they deserve.)

Franz was under no illusion that his death would have any effect upon the war he protested or upon Hitler and the Nazi regime. His witness — and he clearly saw it as such though he never called it that — was to his God and the truth he believed God had entrusted to him. Out of this came the glorious confidence in those last hours that he was already in perfect communication with his Lord. Even had he been forgotten as he came so close to being, it would not lessen the purity or the power of his witness. That it so happened that he was not is more for our benefit than for his, providing an inspiration and challenge for each of us as Christians in these terribly troubled times.

To be true to ourselves and to our God is all that is asked of us. We, too, are called to bear witness, each in his or her own way, in a world ready and armed for that war Thomas Merton warned would be a moral evil "second only to the Crucifixion." Seen in this context the challenges facing us may be even greater than those faced by the Christians under the Third Reich.

Unlike Franz, we need not contemplate the certain loss of our heads for giving witness against policies and programs we know are immoral. For us it is more likely to be a matter of risking inconvenience, of facing scorn or ridicule, or at worst of going to prison. Yet we must protest against the evil others would do in our name or actions they would impose upon us as "duty." In this sense, then, Jaegerstaetter is the true "martyr for our time" whether he is ultimately canonized or not. He serves as the model and patron for all who refuse to violate the dictates of conscience and take a stand, even if forced to stand completely alone.

Not "completely alone" from his perspective. Woven through all the letters to his wife are affirmations of the simple faith that motivated him. Flowers sent to him by his children were placed before a small picture of the Virgin in "one of those little pamphlets about the visitation of the Blessed Mother in Portugal" to make a Mary-shrine in his cell. Repeated requests to be allowed to go to church were regularly denied (because guards could not be spared to accompany him), provoking his comment, "It would not be too much for me if I had to go a hundred kilometers on foot to attend a single Mass, but I guess one must have patience and leave his fate to God to dispose . . . [yet] when I compare my cross and sorrows with the sufferings of others, I must still say that God has always given me the lightest cross to bear." Then, a few weeks later, a jubilant note: "I am as always a child of luck." The reason? Though again denied permission to attend Mass on Easter, he was visited by the prison chaplain in his cell and was able to receive the Sacrament and fulfill his Easter obligation.

This may be the crucial lesson to draw from his story: whatever protest is made, whatever witness we give is incomplete and will be limited in effect unless firmly set in the foundations of a strong religious commitment and open to the graces and blessings provided in the devotions and sacraments which meant so much to him.

Vatican II's *Pastoral Constitution* defines the problem for us: "Men of this generation should realize that they will have to render an account of their warlike behavior; the destiny of generations to come depends largely on the decisions they make today." To guide us in making those decisions, the American bishops in their 1983 peace pastoral call upon us to "have the courage to believe in the bright future and in a God who wills it for us — not in a perfect world, but a better one. The perfect world, we Christians believe, is beyond the horizon, in an endless eternity where God will be all in all. But a better world is here for human hands and hearts and minds to make."

We may not be able to match Franz Jaegerstaetter in courage or piety, but at least we can try to come as close as possible. At the very least his story challenges us to make a sincere re-assessment of our personal commitment as Christians to that "better world" in which peace and justice will reign. Only by so doing can we make certain we will not be numbered among the many who, as Franz put it in another of his commentaries, "still go on living their lives just as though nothing has changed, as if this great and decisive struggle is no concern of theirs."

14.
John Leary:
A Different Sort of Hero

One often hears it said that this is a generation without heroes. Our lives, we are told, have become too tightly organized, too vulnerable to forces and events of which we may not be aware and over which we have little or no control. Social relationships are so complex and impersonal that no single individual, however gifted or committed he or she may be, has the opportunity to influence others or provide the example and leadership that could "change the world." I do not agree.

The real problem is not so much a lack of heroes and the inspiration their lives and actions can provide as it is a failure on our part to recognize them and pay due honor when they do appear in our midst. We blind ourselves with cynicism and construct insurmountable barriers of "practical considerations" against any who would challenge us to break the chains binding us to "the way things are" and shape our lives according to the way things should be. We are uncomfortable with, even a bit embarrassed by, the very thought of heroes and heroism so that on those increasingly rare occasions when we are forced to confront their presence, we escape as quickly as possible by setting them apart and ignoring the meaning they could — and *should* — hold for us and our personal lives.

What makes a hero? Homer sang of Achilles, mightiest warrior of the ancient Greeks, and of his deeds. I will sing my praises of John, the dedicated witness to peace and the nonviolent struggle for social justice. No monuments are likely to be erected to him, no festivals of public homage celebrated in his name, but I count him a hero nonetheless. Wagner's Siegfried, slayer of dragons, was carried on his shield to the funeral pyre in a tumult of crashing chords and cymbals. John lay quietly at rest on his sleeping bag in a simple wood coffin made by his friends and wearing the familiar frayed jacket and cast-off slacks he had found among clothing donated for the poor. For him there was a silence broken only by murmurs of shared grief and smothered sobs of those who dared not trust their voices to speak.

John Timothy Leary, age twenty-four, died suddenly of cardiac arrest in the late afternoon of August 31, 1982. He had finished a full day of work at the Pax Christi Center on Conscience and War and was jogging back to Boston's Haley House, a Catholic Worker soup kitchen where he lived and served the needs of homeless poor and elderly people. Later that evening he was to have attended the regular planning session at Sojourner House, a haven for deserted or displaced families. Following that there was to have been a practice session with the Ailanthus Singers in preparation for the Sunday liturgy. A fairly normal schedule of activity for him; if anything, a lighter day than most.

There is nothing "heroic" about such a death. The same issue of the daily paper which carried his obituary featured the story of another young man crushed by a subway train while trying to rescue a drunken man who had fallen on the tracks. In any contest for the title of "hero of the day" John would not have had a chance. Elsewhere in the world far too many other men, many younger than he, were sacrificing their lives in battle — often in dubious causes. These, too, were far more likely to be hailed as heroes.

The question remains: what makes a hero?

It takes nothing away from those others to answer that heroism, rightly understood, is found not only in how one dies but, even more, in how one lives. To offer tribute to John is to remind ourselves of the goals to which he devoted so much time and youthful energy. In that reminder lies a challenge to ourselves and to all who would honor him to take up the struggle his death left unfinished. It is that challenge which ranks first in importance, but the tribute provides the context which gives the challenge its meaning.

A word of warning is in order. What follows will be no exercise in scholarly detachment and objectivity. Having enjoyed the privilege of knowing and working with this exceptional young man, I make no pretense of being dispassionate about him. Nor do I apologize for the fact. The reader may wish to make allowance for this.

I had high hopes for him. From the vantage point of a half-century in the Catholic peace movement I had come to see in John the talents and commitment that marked him for the leadership that movement will need in the future. Considering all he had already accomplished, it borders on intellectual arrogance for me to speak of him as a "protege"; yet that is how I looked upon him. The reader would do well to make allowance for that too.

But make those allowances with a measure of caution. The unbroken stream of mourners who filed past that simple coffin and the hundreds more who filled Boston's Melkite Cathedral of Our Lady of the Annunciation for the funeral service represented men and women of all ages and every state of life. Street people and "derelicts" who remembered him for his friendly greetings as he served them "on the line" took their place alongside distinguished academics whose classrooms had been brightened by his presence. Distinctions of race and ethnic background lost all significance in the shared misery of an incomprehensible loss.

Differences in religion vanished too. A more ecumenical gathering would be hard to imagine. This devout Catholic who worshiped Sundays in the Byzantine rite of a Melkite congregation and attended daily liturgies in the Latin rite in which he had been baptized and formed had recognized no denominational barriers in his devotion to the one loving God to Whom he had dedicated his life. His labors for peace and justice brought him into close association with believers of virtually every religious persuasion (and a multitude of non-believers as well). They were all there — priests and nuns in abundance mingling with Protestant divines, devout Quakers, Jews, and even a Buddhist monk or two.

All had come to take leave of a young friend and co-worker but, most immediately, for one last glimpse of a warm and universally appealing human being.

Slight of build, lean, not much different in appearance or dress from the ordinary young student "type," John probably would not have attracted any special attention if one passed him on the street. It was in conversation with him, no matter how brief or incidental, that one sensed the qualities which set him apart for those who knew him.

Sister Evelyn Ronan of the Harvard-Radcliffe Catholic Student Center was impressed by what she described as an "incredible combination . . . the boyish, boyish face, and from that boyish face would come a voice with such strength and authority and intelligence." Others, too, were so impressed by the maturity of his thought and manner that they were stunned to learn after his death that he really had been as young as he appeared.

A friend who had shared the experience of being arrested with John wrote of a "mischievous, elfin face; his cheeks curled toward his eyes in ocean waves of smiles as he laughed at ridiculous ideas, though oddly free of sarcasm . . . his habit of holding his hand over his head like a yarmulke when he was making a point, bouncing his hand up and down as if to keep the idea in, like bread in a toaster . . . his energetic nods of agreement, more like bows than nods." Sister Evelyn may be guilty of some exaggeration (though many who knew John will agree) in her final assessment: "You could look into those eyes and see all the way, right into heaven — the goodness was so powerful and the honesty unlike anyone I've ever met."

Exaggeration or not, the impression he left with even the most casual acquaintance was remarkable. One man at the wake had read the obituary in the morning paper and felt he had to come to pay his respects. He had met John but once, a year before, when he stopped to give the young hitchhiker a ride! At that he had the advantage over others who had known him only "second hand" through correspondence or from hearing about him from mutual friends. For them the sense of loss was heightened by not having had the grace of knowing him in person.

John must have been aware of the deep affection he provoked. It would have been enough for him to know he was remembered as a good person, a valued friend, as someone who had been helpful when help was needed. The thought that I or anyone else would offer tribute to him as a "hero" would have struck him as ridiculous enough to set off one of those "ocean waves of smiles."

But, once again, what makes a hero?

If there is a least common denominator, whatever form heroism takes will include the ability to recognize what must be done and the readiness to take personal responsibility for doing it regardless of the risk or cost. That heroic young man crushed by the train met this test in a split moment of decision. For John, on the other hand, meeting it involved endless hours of hard work, intense prayer, and self-denial.

He had heroes of his own, and their example sustained him in his service to the poor and to the cause of peace. One was Franz Jaegerstaetter, the Austrian peasant beheaded in 1943 for refusing to serve in Hitler's army. John drew much spiritual reinforcement from that simple man's willingness to leave wife and children for certain death rather than violate his conscience. In Jaegerstaetter he found a model of the total abandonment to the will of God that characterized his own progress toward the salvation he sought.

Dorothy Day was another source of continuing inspiration. In her unwavering commitment to the spiritual and corporal works of mercy he found the formula for effective Christian witness in a world dominated by inequality and injustice. It was inevitable, given his admiration for this holy old woman, that he became part of Boston's Catholic Worker soup kitchen. His work there was a tangible link to her vision, a vehicle for putting that saving formula into practice.

Then there was Thomas Merton, Trappist monk and leading Catholic apostle of nonviolence. In his spiritual writings, Merton gave expression to the total immersion in the life and love of Christ that motivated John in all his activities.

He made regular personal retreats at the St. Joseph Abbey Trappist monastery in Spencer, MA, evidence that he was attracted to the contemplative life-style which, as Merton demonstrated in his own life and action, could still exert a profound influence upon "the world."

John's studies and spiritual reflection had already convinced him that violence of any kind and in any situation could not be reconciled with the teachings of Christ. In this conviction he recognized an ideological as well as a deep spiritual kinship with Merton.

Jaegerstaetter, witness to the absolute primacy of conscience; Dorothy Day, embodiment of the ideal of sacrificial charity; Merton, prophet of nonviolence. They do not exhaust the list, of course. He was as ecumenical in his intellectual and spiritual attachments as he was in his active associations. Martin Luther King . . . Mohandas K. Gandhi . . . the list could be endless. Taken together they helped define John's personal commitment to social justice and peace. The integration of what he learned from them into a unique and comprehensible life of service to others was his own doing.

There had been hints of this in his early years at home in Connecticut. By the time he was in seventh grade, for instance, his interest in public affairs led to his nomination to the town environmental board. In the 1976 presidential primary he came within two votes of victory as co-ordinator of the Morris Udall campaign. His motivation and ambitions in those years of teenage activity were more political than religious in origin and orientation, but they are evidence that his interest in working for a just social order was already alive and active.

It was Harvard which provided the spark. He had not planned on going there. The youngest son of an Irish-Catholic working-class family, he expected to attend one of the Catholic colleges in the New

England area — assuming, that is, he got to any college at all. His application for admission to the pride of the Ivy League at the urging of a perceptive school counselor was a long-shot gamble as far as he was concerned. Once accepted he resolved to follow through even though, as he would confess, he was not sure he could keep up with the faster intellectual pace he expected to encounter there. He soon proved there was no cause for concern on that score.

Probably the most significant event of his Harvard career was the decision to volunteer for the prison tutoring project conducted by the Phillips Brooks House. This experience sharpened his awareness of the violence and injustice in society and challenged him to accept personal responsibility for doing whatever he could to counteract their destructive effects. He lived in a succession of shared flats and apartments in some of the more depressed neighborhoods of Cambridge and Boston and always made certain the door was open for homeless people he did not know. His prison work continued and expanded and was soon supplemented by an ever-widening involvement in other activities and movements. As the Vietnam controversies broadened into new debates over nuclear disarmament, nuclear energy, American support for oppressive regimes and the like, John was drawn more deeply into a circle of anti-war activities and demonstrations.

At this time, too, he began to play an active part in the anti-abortion movement and was arrested several times for organizing or participating in sit-in demonstrations at abortion clinics. His liberal friends at Harvard and his associates in those other activities may have been shocked and displeased by this "departure from the pattern," but he seems to have won tolerance and respect even from those who disagreed most strongly. He insisted that all the issues involving "respect for life" (including capital punishment as well as war and abortion) were inextricably linked together. In following this course he made it clear that his protests were not judgmental in the sense of condemning the women who believed themselves forced by circumstances to that deplorable decision.

How many he converted to his more comprehensive approach to the so-called "life issues" will never be known. One friend from Phillips Brooks days — writing, as he put it, "in anger at John's God who is sometimes my God as well, and yours and everyone's" — comments on this. "I do not think he was wrong on the abortion issue, even though I disagreed with him completely. In a perfect world (his world), he was right, and I guess that's all that matters." One can almost hear John chuckling in the background, both at his friend's anger and what appears to be a belated change of heart.

Before long he was so deeply involved in so many things that he decided to leave Harvard in his sophomore year. He intended to drop out completely and move to the Washington area to join a community working to organize tenants. He had suddenly realized, as he put it later, ". . . from seven in the morning until one the following morning I was spending all my time calling people or going to meetings or working at the jail. Studies got squeezed in. I couldn't continue that way."

Later that year he thought better of the idea and returned to his studies. Not only would he graduate *magna cum laude* in 1981, but he was chosen by his classmates (in spite of his predictable reluctance to be nominated) to receive Harvard's prestigious Ames Award for service to the greater community. His return did not mean a reduction in the level of outside activity; if anything, his schedule was probably more crowded than before.

My first meeting with John took place in his junior year. He had been taken on as a student intern by the archdiocesan Justice and Peace Commission to assist its Peace Committee I then chaired. One of the tasks for which he volunteered was preparing a slide show on Catholic teachings about war and the arms race. He did an excellent job, but I regret to admit I took little note of him other than to recognize in him a personable, dependable, and exceptionally competent young man. Not until a year or so later, when our mutual involvement in the Center on Conscience and War brought us into much closer association, did I discover the depth and range of his participation in all sorts of local groups and organizations devoted to issues of peace and justice.

At the Center he served as part-time staff but in reality he was much more than that. As one of the Center's founders, he proved in many ways to be its moving spirit, the "glue" which held our operations together. His twenty-hour week at a minimal level of pay grew to at least double that amount (in time, not pay) as he spent evenings representing the organization at meetings of other groups or conducting workshops and giving talks under its auspices.

Ailanthus describes itself as "a nonviolent witness for peace" and John was a devoted participant in its weekly prayer and reflection session. He played a leading part in preparing for its weekly protest vigils at the Draper Laboratories, a Cambridge nuclear weapons research facility. The demonstrators gathered on Monday mornings to greet the Draper employees as they arrived at work and offered them leaflets (some written by John) pointing out the moral implications of their work. On occasion, too, one or more of the demonstrators engaged in civil disobedience by "committing trespass" on the facility's restricted property to distribute their leaflets and pray.

John was arrested twice. For the first offense — not counting his previous anti-abortion sit-ins, of course — he was placed on probation. The second arrest, which he insisted was improper, resulted in the charges being dismissed on a technicality. Neither he nor most of his friends anticipated so happy an outcome and expected that his probation would be canceled and he would end up an inmate at one of the prisons he had served. So sure was he of missing his Commencement on that account, he arranged for someone else to accept the Ames Award for him. In unexpected freedom he was only too delighted to let the substitute arrangement stand. Not much for honors, he welcomed the opportunity to escape.

If Haley House, the Center, and Ailanthus were his "dominant" involvements, one must not ignore the time and energy devoted to other groups and activities in which he took part. A not untypical week in the appointment calendar carried in his ever-present backpack had him attending as many as twenty meetings, over and above the time he spent on the basic three. And these were just the *scheduled* meetings. They did not include a multitude of unrecorded acts of personal chores and favors done for individuals. Friends, neighbors, and just about anyone who needed a few hours of babysitting, a ride to or from the airport, a loan or gift of cash (if he had some handy) knew they could count on John.

Friends, like myself, often cautioned him against the dangers of "overload" and "burn-out" to no avail. Some saw his otherwise inexplicable death as tragic confirmation of their fears. Sister Evelyn goes a step further. "John," she suggests, "had a sensitivity, an awareness of the pain of others that was relentless. Compassion for others had become the dominant experience of his life. I believe he died of an excess of pain."

A stunning hypothesis and not easily dismissed, no matter how difficult it is to reconcile with the bubbling good humor of the young man with whom I shared an office a couple of days a week. If he was suffering from that "excess of pain," he was able to hide it from the rest of us through the sheer joy of his presence. My personal relationship with him was grounded in a mutual respect neither of us felt necessary to put into words, one marked by exchanges of friendly mocking banter. This is always a convenient device for bridging the generation gap, but in this instance it became a game I think we both genuinely enjoyed. I know I did.

I needled him about his frequent retreats, his vegetarianism, his poverty life-style, contrasting it with my enjoyment of bourgeois comforts and the "easier life." He played his part in the "game" with such wit and verve that the all-too-few hours we shared brightened the most dismal day. I miss those exchanges and begrudge the fact those hours were so few. I am sure he understood I was really expressing deep admiration (along with a touch of envy perhaps) for the thoroughness with which he had incorporated into his life and action all the fundamental Christian principles and virtues which others, including myself, find easier to preach than put into actual practice. At least I hope he did.

And *all for the love of God*! How insufferably sanctimonious that pious phrase can be, but in John's case it fits. This is the key to understanding him and everything he did, the essence of his heroism. Fr. Emanuel Charles McCarthy, his spiritual confidant and close friend, made the point in his funeral oration. "Whatever he did in terms of draft counseling, service to the imprisoned, to the hungry, to the homeless, to the unborn was the fruit of the struggle to incarnate, to enflesh, to embody that God that is nonviolent Love." Others recognized this too — in eulogies published in newspapers, in the more than a hundred letters received by his parents.

Boston's diocesan paper, *The Pilot,* put it this way: "If there is a new hunger for justice and peace on this planet, it is because of people like John Leary who stir human hearts with their sheer goodness." To the Rev. Peter Gomes of Harvard's Memorial Church, "the difference with John was that he discovered that life had no purpose, no meaning, no direction, and no focus apart from the purpose and focus of God."

How did he love his God? It would be hard, possibly impossible, to count the ways. But let there be no misunderstanding. This was no "holy Joe" given to public displays of piety; no seeker of converts intruding upon the spiritual privacy of others. John was not the self-righteous type eager to tally the faults and correct the shortcomings of those who do not match or share his own standards of the Good and True. If others sensed his essential goodness and recognized its source in the depth of his faith and the absolute priority he gave it, that was something they discovered on their own. This is not to say that he made any attempt to hide the intensity of his beliefs and devotional practices, nor did he evade religious discussions or demean them by passing them off as abstract discourses on "values" or "philosophy." He may well have been, as one of his distinguished professors said, "the embodiment of the Christian spirit," but he never sought to cultivate that impression in his dealings with others.

It appears this is not the impression one would have drawn from what one friend termed his "wild kid days." By John's own testimony we know that neither external piety nor internal commitment were much in evidence then. Because he was a popular student, successful in studies and track, there is reason to believe he did not remain untouched by the permissive mores and lifestyle of his peers. These qualities, coupled with his handsome features and appealing boyish ways, assured popularity with the young women of his "set" as well as favored status among his pals.

Just how wild those days were is difficult to say. Friends fortunate enough to have been in his confidence freely acknowledge he was certainly no angel.

Indeed, his own later assessment admitted to past personal experiences of which he was not proud and which had taught him not to be harshly judgmental of the weaknesses and misdeeds of others. But whatever escapades or misbehavior may have marred his youthful past were more than compensated for once those "wild kid days" were over. John learned (as we all should know and the lives of so many saints make clear) the lapses of youth, even serious sins, can become the occasion of grace if through repentance and remorse one seeks reconciliation with God and the forgiveness promised by His Son.

One of the failings he confessed was the rejection of the religious practices of his childhood formation, not a rare phenomenon among modern teenagers. In his case the period of alienation was relatively short. But his "return" to the active practice of his Catholic faith was not an uncritical return to the beliefs and pieties of organized religion. Rather it took form as a mature rediscovery and deepening of a spiritual commitment which, however it may have diminished for a time, was never lost. Youthful doubtings, indiscretions, and delinquencies were replaced by an almost compulsive search for opportunities to be of help to others until — again quoting Rev. Gomes — "He became in his short life the complete and total man for others, and those who knew and loved him testify to the love of Christ that shone in and through him."

Only John would know how much time and energy he devoted to prayer and penitential practices. Those retreats of which I made such sport, extended fasts, his daily worship and the special liturgies and commemorative services he organized — all, we may be sure, were but the tip of his devotional iceberg. In a very real sense, every act of service (or protest) was converted into an intimate conversation between him and God. On his bookcase in the room next to the parlor in which his coffin stood was a framed copy of the Prayer of Abandonment of Brother Charles of Jesus. This prayer, perhaps more than anything else, served to set the tone of his days.

If one can speak of a "favorite" prayer, however, it was the Jesus Prayer. Adopting the Eastern practice of continuous prayer which had caught his attention in the course of his religious studies, he recited it literally thousands of times each day: "Lord Jesus Christ, Son of the Living God, have mercy on me, a sinner." If I know John, this was not the mechanical repetition of what too often becomes a mindless fingering of rosary beads; it was, instead, a vehicle for "instant meditation" creating and sustaining the spiritual continuity of his entire day.

I learned of this practice in the course of one of our joking sessions a few weeks before his death. I tried to persuade him to cut down on his running and compared what I called his "scrawniness" with my own "portliness." I told him I had always considered regular exercise of any kind a boring and monotonous waste of time. He laughingly admitted he, too, found jogging boring and monotonous. Then he added that he had overcome both and avoided the waste of time by reciting the Jesus Prayer as he ran along. This means he was probably doing so at the moment of death.

To those of us who share John's religious commitment, such a "happy death" is a blessing and a cause for rejoicing, but that does not relieve the pain of bereavement. We miss him not only as the person we learned to love but, even more, for what he had to offer. His was a very special gift of reconciliation, an ability to bring consensus out of seemingly irreconcilable points of view. Boyish charm and good humor helped, but at its center was a capacity to sense and divert the clash of competing egos and defuse potentially explosive confrontations before contending parties were aware of being on a collision course.

That "angry" Harvard friend described how it worked: "I look back on some of the battles we used to have at Phillips Brooks House over the everyday things. John would speak up softly from some corner of the parlor and smooth everything out. One word of wisdom, softly spoken, genuinely felt, and we all felt such fools (which I guess we really were). His was a sane voice, the right voice, which had no ego driving it, which only had the *love* of everything in it. That's all we needed. We were set back on the right track."

This, I am sure, was an experience shared many times by the other groups of which he was a part. I shared it more than once when John, quiet and inconspicuous somewhere near the foot of the table, would speak the pacifying word.

That commitment to reconciliation carried over to protest actions as well. The resumption of draft registration caused John and some companions to set out to advise young men of the various options open to them. John, of course, took the toughest assignment, leafletting the South Boston post office. Predictably, they were attacked by a band of local toughs intent upon proving their patriotic fervor. Knocked down, kicked and bloodied, he and his companions decided not to press charges. In his letter explaining why, there was no denunciation of the assailants; instead it expressed sorrow for the heavy losses sustained by that community in the Vietnam war and suggested things might have been different had the information John and his friends were trying to provide been available to the young men who had gone before.

That same spirit of reconciliation pervaded leaflets prepared for the Draper vigils. There was no attempt to demean or denounce the employees, only regret for the destructive effects of their efforts. In place of condemnation there was an invitation to reflect upon ways to seek or create a common bond of better understanding. The 1980 Christmas leaflet, written by John, made the point explicit: "Whatever disagreements we may have concerning the right path to peace, we know that it is a value and dream you share with us. We hope that this prayer [of St. Francis of Assisi] will deepen our personal commitment to peace and help open ways for us to work together to eliminate all war, injustice, and fear."

Yet one more time: what makes a hero?

Carl Sandburg, in his monumental biography of Lincoln, draws upon folk wisdom for one of his chapter titles: "A tree is best measured when it is down." Somewhat the same idea can be expressed another way: the beauty that is lost is known and appreciated only in the emptiness of the space the fallen tree had filled.

John met all those other tests of heroism. He dared to take on tasks he knew were beyond his, and probably anyone else's, capacity to complete. He was ready and willing to sacrifice personal comfort and well-being in commitment to those tasks, a commitment reinforced by his complete abandonment to God's will. Nevertheless, it is in the sense of irreparable loss shared by those who had the grace of knowing him for even a little while that his heroism becomes so evident.

"How painful it is," wrote Dan Berrigan, who knew John only from two or three brief meetings, "to try to say 'alleluia' for such a life, given so freely and joyfully to the world's victims in Christ's name. And yet we must do our best."

It is fitting and proper, then, to pay him tribute. But that is not enough.

Doing our best requires something more. On the morning of the funeral a friend took it upon himself to complete John's interrupted run, following the route he had taken to the Haley House destination. That beautiful act of memorial symbolism holds the key to that "something more." It is the challenge John left behind, the work he was unable to finish. Although few will match his achievements or meet the goals he set for himself, each can at least contribute his or her own modest efforts and talents to one or more of the causes he served.

In my own sorrow I have learned to be more aware of what can be done and appreciative of what is being done. It is easy to speak the discouraging word, to bemoan the apathy and indifference of today's youth, to condemn their disregard of traditional religious rules and values. Valid though such complaints may be in general application, they do grave injustice to young people who, like John, are devoting talent and energy to a wide variety of worthwhile causes.

Too often these services go unrecognized and unrewarded. John's death reminded me that one of the rewards of years of activity in the peace movement has been the opportunity to work with such young people, sharing their joy over even minor gains and their disappointment in setback and defeat. In a very real sense what we refer to as "the movement" would not move much at all were it not for those who, like John, were always there to set up the literature tables, rearrange the chairs, run the Xerox, deliver the slides and projector, pick up the leaflets, and then spend hours on some street corner distributing them to usually unreceptive and sometimes abusive passers-by. Not many will be as deeply involved in as many causes as he, but that is simply to say what should be obvious: in the pursuits of peace as in the pursuits of war not everyone is a hero.

Besides, who can tell? Three short years before, I did not suspect that our friendly and cheerful student intern was anyone "special." My attitude toward him, to the extent I had one, was appreciative enough but in a patronizing way. It was good to be able to help someone so intelligent and pleasant meet expenses at college. It was only later, as I studied that appointment book, that I learned to my shame this "nice young kid" was already playing a more active role in the Boston-Cambridge peace community than I.

A few short years. *Only six years in all* since that eighteen-year-old freshman arrived at Harvard charged with vague political ambitions but not quite sure he could make the grade. An incredibly short time to account for the impact he had upon the lives he touched and changed — or the despair and disarray created in those lives when he stumbled to his death. One young woman writes from India that "the whole universe has to make room" for the fact John had died. "I feel such a hole in my heart. My mind keeps wandering to other things and then comes crashing into this: John is dead." To make matters worse there was no one near her who knew him, no one with whom she could share the pain of bereavement. "Who," she asks, "would believe a description of him?"

That is my problem here too. *Who will ever believe?* Most readers by now will have made the allowances I suggested. Some will dismiss my description as an aging man's sentimental indulgence. Others, more charitable, might excuse it as exaggeration, forgivable under the circumstances, but exaggeration nonetheless.

There is one audience, though, for whom this may not be true and it is to them I now turn. Young people whose visions have not yet been warped and dulled by age and experience might understand and accept the possibility that someone like the John I have described could actually exist. They might even be able to identify with him and with what he was trying to do.

That is my hope. Somewhere out there is a host of other young men and women emerging from the unsettled chaos of adolescence and ready to assume the more serious responsibilities and opportunities of adulthood. Some are still in high school and, like John at eighteen, looking forward to college with a mixture of anticipation and concern. Some are already there. They, like John at eighteen, are troubled by what they see as the failure of their parents' generation to deal with poverty, the threat of annihilating war, and all the other evils that plague the society and the world they are about to inherit. Much of their frustration centers upon religion and its exalted preachments about social justice, charity, and peace which so seldom are matched by effective action. So was he. Because of this many have already rejected and turned against their churches or are on the verge of doing so.

This, remember, is where John "was at" when he arrived at Harvard as a freshman eager to get started and yet not quite sure where he was headed or if he would be able to get anywhere at all. If, as he put it later, he never abandoned his belief in God and soon returned to the Church he had left for a time, it was because he discovered there was nowhere else for him to go. So he looked for, and found, a better answer.

It is in that answer that we find the challenge this tribute to John presents. It is a challenge addressed to everyone, but in a very special sense to the young. They, as I said, still have visions, and they have the power and the energy it will take to convert those visions into reality. John discovered that if organized religion, "the Church," had failed it was because individual Christians were failing to live up to its teachings and promise. The solution was obvious: if ordinary Christians began to act as Christians should, "the Church" would come much closer to what he believed it was called to be. As one of those "ordinary" Christians, he took upon himself the obligation to contribute what he could toward achieving that goal — and by so doing provided a model for others to follow now that he is gone.

He had no grandiose dreams of changing the world. It was enough to do what he could to remedy some of its ills and injustices. His modest goal upon graduation from Harvard was "finding people to live with, pray with, and work with, and see what comes from there." What came all too soon, of course, was death. But in that incredibly short span of six years, by his own actions and by inspiring others to take on their share of the task of making Christianity work, he helped us see that to create the better society we seek we must make ourselves better men and women.

That is the challenge. John's death left an opening for a hero, someone to take his place in the struggle for peace and justice. Anyone can apply, male or female . . . any age, though some young person ready and able to pick up where he left off is probably needed most . . . any religion or even none, so long as the commitment is there.

Is this too much to expect? Generations of young people have drawn inspiration from dramatic accounts of valor on the battlefield and gone on to dream dreams of glorious victories to be won and honors to be gained in war. I would place before them this different sort of hero, an eighteen-year-old freshman who in six short years was able to accomplish so much for the twin causes of peace and justice.

The battles he fought had none of the glamour of the mighty contests which bloody the pages of our history books and excite the imaginations of children, making them impatient for the day when they, too, can go forth into glorious combat. John's deeds inspired no headlines; no songs will be sung or holidays proclaimed to mark his victories. But victories they most certainly were.

Homer's Achilles, as is so often the way with heroes of war, celebrated victory by humiliating his vanquished foe, dragging the body behind his chariot around the walls of beleaguered Troy. John Leary's kind of heroism celebrates victory in the restored dignity of the broken and tormented human beings he served. There are people living today because he, or someone like him, was there to give them food. Children who might have perished, physically or psychologically, from neglect survived because he, and others like him, provided shelter and protection. Prisoners live more productive lives because he, and others like him, volunteered to bring them learning and fought for their rights so that life behind bars might be more livable. Some mentally disturbed person wandering the streets of Boston may still treasure the memory of the pleasant young man who took the time to sit and talk with him for a few minutes.

The evils and injustices of society have not diminished to any great extent; if anything, they seem to be increasing. At least John Leary was there to help where help was needed and, equally important, to leave with those he helped the gift of hope. And this was possible because out of his own complete personal commitment to his God he was able to draw hope in sufficient abundance to share. Men he helped gain discharge from military service they had come to see as sinful testify to their debt to him. Draft resisters and conscientious objectors found encouragement and strength in his quiet assurances. I suspect there may even be employees at Draper Lab or at some abortion clinic who find themselves troubled from time to time because of that friendly young man who once handed them a leaflet.

On second thought, John's death leaves an opening for a multitude of heroes in the struggle for peace and justice. One replacement is probably not enough to fill the gap.

The well-known Christopher motto may have become a pious cliche, but it is true nonetheless. It *is* better to light a single candle than to curse the darkness. John Leary went about lighting candles all over the place. With his passing they are slowly flickering out. Not completely, though. Their brightness continues in the candles others are lighting in his memory and in their determination that what he began must not, and will not, go unfinished by default. If the "encircling gloom," as the familiar old hymn has it, is deeper now without his presence among us, each candle lit will seem to burn all the brighter.

Perhaps this tribute will inspire one young person enough to accept the challenge John left and reach for a match to light his or her own. If so, it will have served its purpose.

One would wish, of course, for many more.

Sources

The following are the original citations for essays included in this collection. There has been minor editing for reasons of style, to minimize repetition, to make the expression more contemporary. None of the changes, however, have affected the substance of the positions taken or the arguments presented in their support.

Chapter 1: The Christian Vocation of Peace
Originally published in *Ave Maria*, March 23, 1968.

Chapter 2: The Church and the Arms Race
Originally an address presented January 13, 1978, at the Second Pax Christi Bishops' Day of Peace in Newark; the text was published in the May 1978 issue of the *Catholic Worker*.

Chapter 3: Catholic Opposition to Hitler: The Perils of Ambiguity
Originally published in the Autumn 1971 issue of the *Journal of Church and State*.

Chapter 4: Total War and "Absolute" Pacifism
Originally published in *Concilium* (c.1982). I have reprints from that international journal in English, German, Dutch and French. None have exact date of issue.

Chapter 5: Peace, War, and the Christian Conscience
Originally a London talk marking the 50th anniversary of the British Pax Society. This abbreviated version appeared in *New Blackfriars*, June 1987 issue.

Chapter 6: Catholic Responses to the Holocaust
Originally published in the June 1981 issue of *Thought*.

Chapter 7: A Religious Pacifist Looks at Abortion
Originally published in *Commonweal* (May 28, 1971).

Chapter 8: The Burden of Liberation: A Pacifist Reflection
Originally published in the March 1977 issue of *Worldview.*

Chapter 9: In Our Image
Originally published in *Commonweal* (June 19, 1959).

Chapter 10: Memories of Warner
Originally published in the October-November 1977 issue of the *Catholic Worker.*

Chapter 11: The Berrigans: Radical Pacifism Personified
Originally published in the December 1970 issue of *The Catholic World*; reprinted in William VanEtten Casey's *The Berrigans* (1971); also in *Dissent.*

Chapter 12: Thomas Merton: Nonviolence and the Spirituality of Peace
Originally given as a paper at a conference on Spirituality at St. John's University (Collegeville, MN); published in the second quarter issue of *Cistercian Studies,* 1985.

Chapter 13: Franz Jaegerstaetter: Martyr for Conscience
Originally published as a Pax Christi USA "Peacemaker's" Pamphlet, 1984. Signed copies of *In Solitary Witness: The Life and Death of Franz Jaegerstaetter* are available($10.95, plus $2) from the Center on Conscience and War, which also distributes videotape copies of *The Refusal,* the Austrian film based on the book. For information, write Gordon C. Zahn, 780 Boylston, 26D, Boston, MA 02199.

Chapter 14: John Leary: A Different Sort of Hero
Original title, "Requiem for a Young Hero: A Tribute and a Challenge," published in 1983 with other memorial writings (including a poem, "Journey to Block Island" by Dan Berrigan) by the Center on Conscience and War. Now available as a Pax Christi USA "Peacemaker's" Pamphlet.